THE SECRETS OF
F R A N K   H E R B E R T ' S
DUNE™

Text by
JAMES VAN HISE

DVD Produced by
MICHAEL D. MESSINA

www.scifi.com/dune

ibooks

DISTRIBUTED BY SIMON & SCHUSTER

An Original Publication of ibooks, inc.

Copyright © 2000 by Victor Television Productions, Inc.

An ibooks, inc. Book

Distributed by Simon & Schuster, Inc.
1230 Avenue of the Americas, New York, NY 10020
ibooks, inc.
24 West 25th Street
New York, NY 10010

The ibooks World Wide Web Site Address is:
http://www.ibooksinc.com

ISBN 0-7434-0730-X
First ibooks printing November 2000
10 9 8 7 6 5 4 3 2 1
SCI FI Channel and colophon are registered trademarks of the SCI FI Channel.

NEW AMSTERDAM and colophon are registered trademarks of
New Amsterdam Entertainment, Inc.

Editor: Dwight Jon Zimmerman
Cover design by Mike Rivilis
Interior design by Mike Rivilis and Gilda Hannah

Printed in the U.S.A.

CONTENTS

FRANK HERBERT'S

DUNE™

THE SCI FI CHANNEL PRESENTS

A NEW AMSTERDAM® ENTERTAINMENT, INC. PRODUCTION

IN ASSOCIATION WITH VICTOR TELEVISION PRODUCTIONS, INC. & BETAFILM GmbH

WILLIAM HURT IN FRANK HERBERT'S DUNE

STARRING ALEC NEWMAN GIANCARLO GIANNINI UWE OCHSENKNECHT IAN McNEICE

BARBORA KODETOVA P.H. MORIARTY JULIE COX LASLO IMRE KISCH

WITH MATT KEESLAR AS FEYD AND SASKIA REEVES AS JESSICA

CASTING BY MOLLY LOPATA, C.S.A. MUSIC BY GRAEME REVELL VISUAL EFFECTS SUPERVISOR ERNEST FARINO

EDITED BY HARRY B. MILLER, III COSTUME DESIGNER THEODOR PISTEK PRODUCTION DESIGNER MILJEN "KREKA" KLJAKOVIC

CINEMATOGRAPHY VITTORIO STORARO A.I.C. A.S.C. PRODUCED BY DAVID KAPPES

EXECUTIVE PRODUCERS RICHARD P. RUBINSTEIN & MITCHELL GALIN

WRITTEN FOR THE SCREEN AND DIRECTED BY JOHN HARRISON

Richard P. Rubinstein, John Harrison and William Hurt

FOREWORD
RICHARD P. RUBINSTEIN
Executive Producer

I would have never thought that I would embrace television the way I have because I started off as a feature film producer. But while my back was turned, television grew up. In addition, I learned from my experience with Stephen King's "The Stand" that the mini-series format is a major asset for adapting a long complicated novel into a movie. I know writer/director John Harrison felt that way when he adapted *Dune* into a screenplay for a 6-hour mini-series.

My relationship with *Dune* began as a reader in the late 60s. It was one of my favorite novels. When I saw the Dino De Laurentiis produced feature adaptation I did not feel like it captured the soul of the book. However, it wasn't until almost 15 years later that I began to try to do something about giving the novel a second chance on screen. One night, around four o'clock in the morning, I was looking at my "first edition" bookshelf, and my eye gravitated to the spine of *Dune*. I wondered if I could get the TV rights and produce a mini-series version of the book. The next day I went into the office and found out that there was an

Richard P. Rubinstein and John Harrison

ongoing dispute in terms of who owned the television rights. Literally the day that the dispute was resolved was the day that I approved an agreement with the Frank Herbert estate to option the TV rights to Dune and its 5 sequel books.

Even though *Dune* has received great acclaim as a science fiction novel, it is much more than a science fiction story. Readers or viewers can experience *Dune* on several different levels having little to do with science in the future. There are universal and powerful themes in "Frank Herbert's Dune" relating to love, loyalty, and a young man coming of age. *Dune* is also a big action/adventure epic in the tradition of *Lawrence of Arabia*. This is not to suggest that we've forgotten the high tech and monster fans since "Frank Herbert's Dune" has some knockout special effects including the giant worms that guard the spice.

The budget for this mini-series was more than $20 million dollars. It sounds like a lot of money, but given what we wanted to achieve, it wasn't as much as you might think. A great portion of *Dune* is set on the desert world of Arrakis. It wasn't until after I spent several days in the Namibian desert where the wind was a steady forty-five miles an hour that I realized you can't be out in that kind of environment and not have sand get into everything. That kind of experience led us to focus on the practical difficulties of filming in the desert. We looked at our budget and thought, "Can we afford to be sitting doing nothing for three days if the wind comes up?" We didn't think so. John Harrison then embraced an interior/exterior concept where we would create a unique desert uni-

Richard P. Rubinstein and Vittorio Storaro

verse for "Frank Herbert's Dune" on very large soundstages. Mitchell Galin, David Kappes, and John then found Prague's Barrandov Studios fit the bill.

As the senior Executive Producer, I try to maintain a day to day distance creatively after the birth of the project. This approach allows me to have some perspective and overview during the editing of the movie but puts more importance on having the right director and creative team in the first place. After you see the mini-series, I believe you will feel that my faith in John Harrison, Vittorio Storaro, Theodor Pistek, Miljen "Kreka" Kljakovic, Ernest Farino and Harry Miller among many others was justified. On the producing side I was lucky to have my co-executive producer, Mitchell Galin to represent us in the development of the script and during casting. On a day to day basis I slept well because David Kappes was in Prague running the production.

With respect to the cast I've said facetiously that we're not holding it against certain actors that their names are well known. That wasn't why they were hired. John's first focus was getting the right actors and I felt he was very successful. John also had the freedom to use more new faces than usual because *Dune* itself is a well-recognized "brand name" novel and a star in its own right.

I had good timing when it came to finding a TV home for *Dune*. The SCI FI Channel had decided to make a big statement about its commitment to original programming. Their problem was finding a program that appealed to the SCI FI Channel's core audience, but also reached out

to a broader range of viewers. They saw in *Dune* the same general audience appeal that I did.

I am very grateful to the past and present execs at the SCI FI Channel and USA Networks, to New Amsterdam's corporate partner, ABC, and to our international partner, Betafilm of Munich, for giving us enough rope to hang ourselves. I hope *The Secrets of Frank Herbert's Dune* will give you a feel for how we avoided the gallows. This book can't ever stand in for the mini-series itself, but it does give you a view from behind the camera.

My heartfelt thanks go out to all who helped make it happen including the legions of fans of Frank Herbert's novel that told us they were ready for another adaptation.

New York City
July 2000

John Harrison

"FRANK HERBERT'S DUNE"
THE STORY, THE CAST, THE CREW
By Director John Harrison

Three years ago Richard P. Rubinstein and Mitchell Galin came to me and said that they'd acquired the television rights to Frank Herbert's novel *Dune* and would I be interested in writing and directing a mini-series based on it. Richard, Mitchell and I had collaborated successfully many times in the past, both in features and television. I knew we could do it again with this material. An opportunity like this comes along infrequently if ever in one's career, and I saw in "Frank Herbert's Dune" an extraordinary opportunity to unite a much-loved and renowned piece of literature with some of the finest filmmaking talents in the business; a chance to create unique and memorable television. How could I not take this project on? I was sure that we could do something with it that hadn't been done previously.

So, after a moment's pause (so as not to appear too greedy) I asked how fast I could sign up? Like many of my generation, I'd read the book when I was young and was strongly influenced by it. Reading *Dune* wasn't simply an exercise in fun reading; it was a serious, often difficult encounter with ideas, political, social and religious. The chance to translate those ideas to a broad medium like television was both exciting and challenging.

Duke Leto (*William Hurt*)

I spent several weeks reading and re-reading Herbert's book, analyzing the characters, the story, making notes on each chapter, trying to outline the action in each one, but most importantly the theme of each. Because in the end, *Dune* is not simply a book of plot and adventure, it's a book of philosophy.

I believed from the start that the story of *Dune* could be accessible even to a wide audience; that even people who might never pick up a science-fiction book could understand and embrace it. After all, it's a classic myth-story: A young man, Paul Atreides, is uprooted from his cherished homeland, taken by his beloved and honorable father to a distant and dangerous planet to start a new life. But jealous enemies assassinate the father and the son is left with his mother to die in the brutal, merciless wilderness. Adopted by seemingly primitive indigenous tribes, the young man learns their ways, adopts their customs, and eventually fulfills the promise of their legends and becomes their Mah'di, their messiah. In so doing, he learns the truth about himself and the meaning of his life. Through that odyssey of his own spirit, the young prince leads the desert tribes to freedom and rids the universe of the corruption that is pulling it apart. But such victory is never that neat and easy. The young prince's triumph sets off a chain of events not even he can control. The saga of *Dune* doesn't end. It grows.

A classic story. A fable. A cautionary tale. The stuff of myth.

I decided that Herbert's own structure could serve quite well as the basis for the mini-series. Each night would reflect one of the three "books" that comprise his novel: "Dune," "Muad'dib," and "The Prophet." Night One, therefore, would be the story of the Atreides family and the vicious, complex conspiracies against it. Night Two would be the story of Paul surviving his family's defeat, learning the ways of the desert. And finally, Night Three would be Paul's emergence as the Fremen Mah'di, the messiah that would lead them to victory and freedom, the leader who struggles under the yoke of his own destiny. And tying it all together would be the mystical odyssey of Paul towards the enlightenement to which he was fated.

Paul Atreides (*Alec Newman*)

Saskia Reeves and John Harrison

I was determined to be as faithful as possible to Frank Herbert's novel. And after about six months I had completed the story adaptation and the over 300-page screenplay. Now of course, novels and television are two different mediums. So there had to be certain adaptations. The narrative structure, for example, had to be more linear. Some subplots had to be subsumed into others. Some characters would never get the detailed attention they got in the novel. But I think those who know the book well will see that what we've accomplished is an honest and scrupulous adaptation of Frank Herbert's novel.

Now it was up to Richard and Mitchell to put together the production. And it wasn't easy. But, thankfully, their dedication and perseverance even during the most difficult periods finally paid off and we headed to Europe to start facing the myriad decisions that would have to be made. With the uncompromising help and patient management skills of David Kappes, our producer, we were able to assemble an army of first-

Dr. Kynes (*Karel Dobry*)

rate artists and technicians to bring this novel to life and deliver production values exceeding expectations.

To me, *Dune* is an adventure novel. It is called sci-fi but I think of it as speculative fiction, a romantic epic in the classic tradition. When we decided to investigate the possibility of creating a completely fantasy-oriented unvierse primarily on sound stages in Europe, I was adamant that we not do it as a "green screen" show. By that I mean I didn't want to create an environment that had one or two props and the rest of the room simply key green backdrops into which we'd "paint" computer-generated environments. I didn't feel this method would allow us to accurately portray the world I wanted to see, and secondly I didn't want the actors performing in a reference-less vacuum. Instead, I was lucky enough to get two wonderful artists to help me create a marvelously unique vision of "Frank Herbert's Dune," Production Designer Miljen "Kreka" Kljakovic and Cinematographer Vittorio Storaro.

Gurney Halleck (*P.H. Moriarty*)

I had been a fan of Kreka's work for many years, going back to his films *Delicatessen* and Kusturica's *The Underground.* During a scouting trip through North Africa and Europe, I veered off to Paris where he lives to seduce him into designing the mini-series for me. We agreed right away that to make such a project work we'd need specific and remarkable identities for each of the specific environments of "Frank Herbert's Dune." These locales included the Imperial planet of the Emperor, the dark planet where Baron Harkonnen lives, and of course, the desert planet Arrakis, also called *Dune*, wasteland of the empire. Home of the Spice. Home of the mysterious Fremen. I wanted everyone watching the mini-series to understand instantly the cultural difference between these worlds and communities.

I was introduced to Vittorio Storaro by my talented, resourceful right-hand man, Assistant Director Matt Clark. Turns out this master of light had long loved Herbert's novel. He'd almost worked on Jodoworski's ill-fated attempt to produce a movie of *Dune* in the 70s, and had been approached again by Ridley Scott during another effort to bring Herbert's novel to film. When he heard that I was doing a new version, a longer version to truly capture the book, he asked to meet me. It

Princess Irulan (*Julie Cox*)

Feyd (*Matt Keeslar*) and Baron Harkonnen (*Ian McNeice*)

was like a dream come true for me, of course. I'd been studying Vittorio's work for years, stealing his ideas, his styles, in even the simplest of my TV work. I knew if I could get him to shoot this production of "Frank Herbert's Dune," we would have a striking and memorable picture. Sure enough, the evidence is now there for everyone to enjoy. Not only did Vittorio create an incredible, thoughtful and detailed color scheme for every aspect of the mini-series, emotionally and philosophically he helped design and execute the magnificent Translites that complimented Kreka's production design. Created and rendered with computer graphics by Fabrizio Storaro, these Translites are as large as one hundred feet by thirty feet and covering the entire length of the biggest soundstage in Europe. They allowed me to create environments we never could have had anywhere on location. Sietch Tabr, for example, the primary home

Stilgar (*Uwe Ochsenknecht*)

of Stilgar's Fremen tribe deep in the desert on Dune. Kreka, Vittorio and I spent many hours pondering what such a sietch would look like. From the start, I was determined to exhibit the rich cultural life of the Fremen, which is described in great detail in the book. Their desert communities had to visually represent that sophisticated culture. With Vittorio and Kreka's unyielding encouragement, I settled on a look that was inspired by the mysterious and haunting temples of Petra in Jordan, the esthete

Paul Atreides, Duke Leto and Dr. Kynes

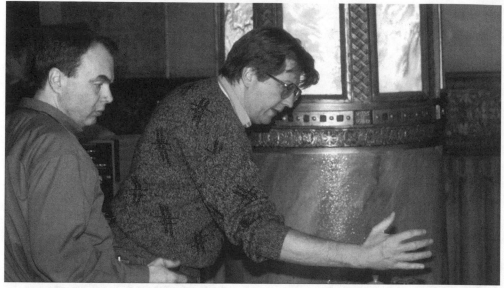

John Harrison and Ernest Farino

communities of the Essenes, and the Holy Land paintings of David Roberts.

Like the production design, I wanted a costume design that was instantly recognizable and stunning. When I came to Prague, I knew of the designer, Theodor Pistek, who had won an Academy Award for

Vittorio Storaro

Amadeus. I also knew that he is a national treasure in the Czech Republic. We'd be lucky just to have an interview with him. When I told him about "Frank Herbert's Dune," he wasn't much interested in the job because he's not a fan of science fiction. But I said, "No, no. This is not sci-fi. This is epic adventure. It's classic storytelling, and we have a terrific opportunity to break the mold here. I want you to think of this as Shakespeare . . . as Mallory. I want you to consider a kind of Oriental/Arab/Medieval European design concept . . . because I think Herbert's novel is infused with ideas and images from all these."

Luckily Theodor became intrigued, and within a week, I had a pile of phenomenal drawings for all the principal characters. Then we started working with Vittorio in terms of color schemes. Like the production design, every wardrobe identifies the world that we're in. Each one gives you a psychological insight into the character, the tribe and the culture with which we're dealing.

The final pieces of the creative puzzle fell into place when Ernie

Left to right: Count Fenring (*Miroslav Taborsky*), Emperor Shaddam IV (*Giancarlo Giannini*) and Reverend Mother Mohiam (*Zuzana Geislerová*)

Farino agreed to handle the visual effects and Harry Miller joined me to edit this epic. Having worked with both many times, I knew the great burden of pulling this six-hour leviathan together was in great hands.

Ernie was integrally involved with Kreka, Vittorio and myself designing every one of the visual effects in this production. Everything from set extensions to worm attacks. Everything from crowd replication to Heighliners folding space. Without his expert collaboration day in and day out we would have been lost and the scope of "Frank Herbert's Dune" would have been lost. Furthermore, Ernie took on the difficult task of directing the 2nd unit.

Having cut several pictures together already, I knew that Harry Miller would be able to manage the enormous challenges of this story-telling. He was in Prague for the entire production, cutting as we shot, so that I could visit on weekends and see how we were doing. Because

A Fremen girl

Above left to right: Stilgar, Duke Leto, Duncan Idaho (*James Watson*) and Thufir Howat (*Jan Vlasák*). Bottom left to right: Reverend Mother Ramallo (*Drahomira Fialkova*) and Chani (*Barbora Kodetová*)

he knew my rhythms, my style, he was able to present me with finely-tuned scenes. Many were the day I looked to Harry to solve a dramatic problem with his editing skills. And as we've had to make the inevitable adjustments to structure and pacing, Harry's keen storytelling sense has been invaluable.

So now the creative team behind the camera was complete. All we needed was a world-class cast to bring the mini-series to life.

When we were talking about casting "Frank Herbert's Dune," we had to make a choice. Either go after certain stars and try drawing an audience by virtue of their names, or go with gifted talent that would be right for each role regardless of how well-known. My instinct is always to go with great actors, and if they are unknown, so be it. After all, the real star in this case is the story of *Dune*. So I was insistent that we find the best actor for each of the roles. Luckily for me, everyone agreed that a production of "Frank Herbert's Dune" cries out for an international cast. Actors of different cultures and backgrounds could only enhance the different worlds of the story. I was lucky to have found an ensemble of gifted talent to bring each role to life.

Almost immediately I was presented with an opportunity I couldn't resist. William Hurt wanted to play Duke Leto. Like so many of the rest of us involved in this project, William had always loved Herbert's novel. When we met in New York City, I knew I'd found Duke Leto. Continuing long distance conversations while he was on other locations and I was in pre-production only reinforced my enthusiasm.

John Harrison and Theodor Pistek

I love working with actors. I love the process of discovering who the character is. In television, one has precious little time to explore such issues, let alone rehearse them. But the degree of intelligence, of commitment, of depth William was willing to bring to a character that is essentially murdered and removed from the story early on, was truly gratifying to me. Because of it, Leto's spirit infuses the remainder of Paul's journey through nights Two and Three as if he were still on the scene.

The major challenge of "Frank Herbert's Dune" was finding the right person to play the lead, Paul Atreides. In the book Paul is introduced at age fifteen and we see him age a few years over the course of the story. The talent pool in this age range is woefully shallow. I knew we'd have to cast someone older and find someone with the range to pull off everything from the ambivalence and angst of a teenager to the mature, desert-hardened fanaticism and charisma of a legend. It wouldn't be easy. With Molly Lopata, our casting director, I looked everywhere. Finally (and almost by accident), I found Alec Newman, a brilliant young Scot who had the energy, the look, the intensity to become Paul Muad'dib. Our first meeting was late at night in a hotel lobby; not the most inspiring place for an actor to show his wares or a director to judge them. But something about Alec wouldn't leave me alone, and after that meeting I felt convinced that I'd found the right actor for Paul. It was a stroke of great luck. Or maybe it was meant to be. Maybe he *was* the Muad'dib waiting to happen.

Barbora Kodetová, Richard P. Rubinstein and John Harrison

Ian McNeice and John Harrison

In England I also found Saskia Reeves, a renowned British Theater actress, to play Paul's mother, Lady Jessica. I'd looked far and wide for somebody who would have the *gravitas*, the sensitivity and the emotional warmth to play Lady Jessica. I saw an audition tape of hers in which she did a half-hour monologue about killing her mother. It was an extraordinarily compelling performance. Everything I'd been looking for was exhibited in this monologue. But like all the other actors in "Frank Herbert's Dune," Saskia is extremely thoughtful and deliberate. It took many long and heartfelt conversations to convince her she could be a great Jessica. In the end, she proved it.

In the novel, Princess Irulan is simply the biographer/narrator of much of the story. But those who know the *Dune* mythology understand that she plays a significant character in the continuing drama. She couldn't simply be a cipher that would appear in the final scenes, a mere device for Paul to checkmate the Emperor. I needed someone who could take the character I gleaned from Irulan's writings and create a memorable persona. I found that someone in Julie Cox, also from London. A gifted and beautiful young actress, Julie has taken Irulan and given her a life that was only hinted at in the novel.

Uwe Ochsenknecht is a wonderfully intense and complex actor from Germany, a big star in Europe, whose talents range from serious drama to hilarious comedy. Perfect for the complexity of Silgar, I thought. Like the others, Uwe was a fan of the book and he came to me with wonderfully developed ideas of how to make Stilgar human and compelling.

I was introduced to Barbora "Bara" Kodetova via a short film of one

Lady Jessica and Paul Atreides

of Strindberg's plays. The entire piece was essentially Bara's monologue, and it was so moving I couldn't take my eyes off it. Furthermore, Bara comes from a family of great Czech actors, and she has the spirit, the passion, the physicality to play Chani, the great love of Paul Muad'dib.

Giancarlo Giannini came from Italy to play the Emperor. I was thrilled when he agreed to take the part. Giancarlo is known for his great romantic and comic performances. But few outside Italiy realize that he is one of the finest Shakespearean actors that country has produced. The day he walked on the set in his first wardrobe, as Shaddam IV, his presenced proclaimed, "I am the Emperor."

Ian McNeice who plays Baron Harkonnen lives in Los Angeles. Molly Lopata introduced me to him and he did one of the most outrageous auditions I have ever seen. Whenever you write a scene you obviously have a certain image of that character in your mind, and it's incredibly wonderful to find an actor who takes the image that you have, becomes it and takes it even further. That's what Ian McNeice did with the Baron, and he continued to surprise me with all of the wonderful things he brought to the role. William Hurt told Ian that he was born to play this role.

I was introduced to P.H. Moriarty, who plays Gurney Halleck, by David Kappes, who had worked with him on a previous film. P.H. began his acting career working with Bob Hoskins on *The Long Good Friday*, and I met him almost as a courtesy to David. But once I saw him, I knew that this guy was Gurney Halleck. He has an eye that was damaged earlier in his life, which, having added the scar that Gurney Halleck has, makes his face so expressive and so intense.

I'd seen Matt Keeslar, who plays Feyd, in a couple of films and I thought this is a really interesting young actor, but I didn't know too much about him. My friend Wes Craven did *Scream 3* with him and thought he did a terrific job. When he was suggested to me I thought, well, he's kind of an emerging young star. Maybe he won't want to come over and do "Frank Herbert's Dune" in the Czech Republic for four months. But he wanted to do it right away, so we snatched him up and he's delightfully evil.

I believe that the story of *Dune* is in many ways more relevant today than it was when Herbert wrote it. The world in which we live now is far closer to the universe he created than the bi-polar Cold War of the Fifties and Sixties. I consider it my good fortune and enormous responsibility to have had this chance. I also realize that without the collaboration of the people I've mentioned here, and the countless others I haven't (but whose work is all over this production), "Frank Herbert's Dune" could not have been made. For their efforts, their friendship and help to remain true to the spirit of Frank Herbert's monumental work at the same time we fashioned an accessible and entertaining filmed adventure, I'm extremely grateful.

THE PLAYERS

Paul Atreides

Duke Leto and Lady Jessica

HOUSE ATREIDES

L ed by Duke Leto Atreides, House Atreides is one of the Great Royal
Houses of the Imperium. These Royal Houses comprise one arm of
a tenuously balanced trilogy of power with the Emperor and the
Navigators of the Spacing Guild comprising the others.

The balance of power among the Houses appears to shift in favor of
House Atreides when Duke Leto is ordered by the Emperor to replace
House Harkonnen and oversee the production of "Spice," a life-sustain-
ing substance found only on the planet Arrakis (called "Dune" by its
native inhabitants). Spice is the most precious commodity in the universe. It is believed among the Houses that he who controls the Spice
controls the Empire. But when Leto is betrayed by one of his own, a dev-
astating conflict with the rival Harkonnen ensues. The Duke's son, Paul,
and his mother, Jessica, a magical Bene Gesserit witch with powers of
mind control, must escape into the desert. Under his mother's tutelage,
Paul hones his own considerable Bene Gesserit gifts, begins to see into
the future and realize his far-reaching ability to shape it.

Academy Award winner William Hurt plays Duke Leto in the mini-
series. Born March 20, 1950, his first starring role in a feature was in the

Duke Leto

science fiction film *Altered States* (1980) which featured a mind-bending story and state-of-the-art special effects. Other major roles soon followed in a variety of films including *The Big Chill* (1983), *Gorky Park* (1983), *Kiss of the Spider Woman* (1985), *Children Of A Lesser God* (1986), *Broadcast News* (1987), *The Accidental Tourist* (1987), and the science fiction films *Until the End of the World* (1991), *Dark City* (1998) and *Lost in Space* (1998).

"As far as Duke Leto is concerned," Hurt stated, "he's a man who is struggling with his destiny. Leto's very aware of the trap that he's in."

William Hurt was familiar with Dune even before the previous filmed version was made. "I first read it not long after it came out—the late sixties or early seventies—and it grabbed me." He said. "I was a science fiction junkie for a long time. What I loved about Dune was that it talked about human politics and the human search for something better."

William Hurt was pleased with how the production came together. "I've really enjoyed it," he said. "I think we're very lucky to have John Harrison as our director. He's chosen some wonderful actors and gives them room to work. I'm amazed by the generosity of the producers and the director to let us find the scenes this way. It just gives you tremendous amounts of energy, and ideas."

Duke Leto's son, Paul, is the central character of the story. Paul is played by Alec Newman. Alec was born November 27, 1974 in Glasgow, Scotland. Initially, Alec has worked mostly on the stage, however his previous film roles prior to "Frank Herbert's Dune" were in *Rag Nymph* (1997) and *Greenwich Mean Time* (1999). In describing his young co-star,

Duke Leto and Duncan Idaho

William Hurt stated, "I identify a lot with him. It's not hard to care about him. He's a very generous and a very conscientious actor. It takes a lot of stamina to handle something like this. He is very sturdy and talented. It's hard to find those combinations of sturdiness and great talent. You look at him and you go, *I can't think of anybody other than him to play Paul Atreides*."

Unlike William Hurt, Alec Newman said, "Before I met John Harrison to talk about the part, I really didn't know *Dune* at all. After I read the script, I realized that it's really a very human story and it has all the elements of the human world. It's really exciting visually. It's about religion. It's about politics. About social order. There's a debate about morality. They're really well laid out in the book and in John Harrison's

William Hurt

script. Although *Dune* is set in the far distant future, it feels like you're really dealing with a story that has a kind of historical feel."

"From the very word go I realized that whatever else Paul Atreides is—the *Kwisatz Haderach* foretold by the Bene Gesserit or the Mah'di—the messiah of the Fremen," Alec said, "he is a human being. Paul actually spends a lot of time in the story reacting in a very human way to what people say he is. He reacts with fear, trepidation, and doubt. Then there's a very slow realization of what he is and what destiny has chosen for him. Paul spends a lot of time resisting his destiny until he realizes he actually is this messiah-like figure."

Working on "Frank Herbert's Dune" also required that he train in the use of weapons and have some action scenes.

Paul Atreides

"I really enjoyed it, so I probably was a bit too much into it. I'd been lucky enough to have had some stage combat training in drama school in London with broadswords and sabers and unarmed combat, so first reading through the script of 'Frank Herbert's Dune' I thought, *Great, there's a scrap there! That'll be fun.* Actually, it's been a lot more challenging than I ever anticipated. I don't know what I would have done if I hadn't been already trained reasonably well.

"Peter Drozda, the stunt coordinator is quite a character. I wouldn't mess with him because I think with one hand he can throw me and six other guys all over a wall without even thinking about it. He used to be an Olympic wrestler."

The camaraderie Alec felt extended to his experience working with

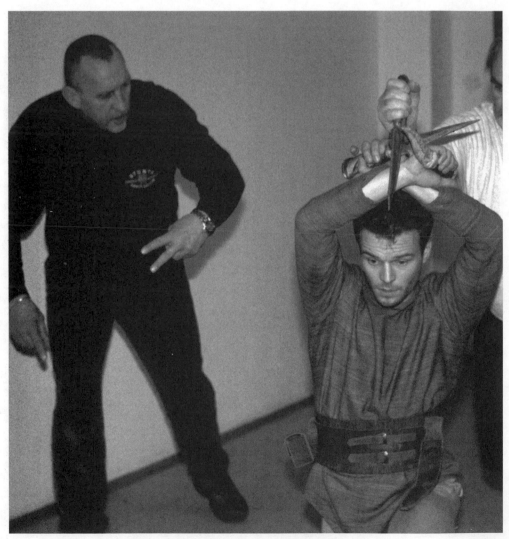

Stunt Coordinator Peter Drozda, Alec Newman and P.H. Moriarty

Paul Atreides

director John Harrison. "The great thing about working with John is his imagination," said Alec. "I really trust it. He's very much an actor's director. He manages to keep everything happening through his passion for the story."

Jessica Atreides, the "bound concubine" of Duke Leto, is portrayed by Saskia Reeves, an English actress. "Jessica Atreides has quite an interesting journey herself," said Saskia. "She has gone against the very thing she'd been bred to do [have an Atreides daughter] because of her enor-

Paul Atreides

Lady Jessica and Paul Atreides

Lady Jessica

mous love for Duke Leto. Her journey is the story of what happens because of her decision to give Leto the son he desired. The decision has resonance. It's a very good story."

Saskia Reeves has appeared in a number of movies prior to co-starring in "Frank Herbert's Dune." Her film work includes *A Woman Of Substance* (1984), *Close My Eyes* (1990), *The Bridge* (1990), *December Bride* (1990), *Antonia And Jane* (1991), *In The Border Country* (1991), *Butterfly Kiss* (1994), *Traps* (1994), *I.D.* (1995), *The Perfect Match* (1995), *Different For Girls* (1996), *Heart* (1998), and *L.A. Without a Map* (1998).

Although principal photography took more than four months, and Jessica's scenes were filmed throughout, Saskia found that director John Harrison made the work go smoothly.

"He's a very nice man. I'm curious as to how he keeps his sense of humor under such stressful conditions. He's great company. Very patient, and he's been a good friend. I don't think this shoot would have been as happy as it is if he hadn't been directing it. You can always talk to him. He's that way with every single person on the crew; accessible to us all."

She also spoke highly of her co-stars, Alec Newman and William Hurt. "I work more with them than with anybody else. We've become very good friends and that's reflected in our working relationship. It's been wonderful."

Saskia also found it special to work with one of her former drama teachers, Ian McNeice, who plays the lead villain, Baron Harkonnen

"Ian was with the William Shakespeare Company and the drama school I was at would encourage professional actors to direct the students in their final year of drama school. Ian and I worked together on a couple of plays. Ian is an amazing character and a wonderful person, so to finally get to work together professionally has been a real treat."

Matt Keeslar, Peter Drozda and Alec Newman

Baron Harkonnen

Feyd

HOUSE HARKONNEN

An epic story needs villains and the House Harkonnen, led by Baron Vladimir Harkonnen fits the bill perfectly. The Harkonnens have hated House Atreides and have sought their downfall for ages. Their crusade to bring down the Atreides forms the counterpoint to the rise of Paul Atreides and the ascendance of his family.

The Harkonnen live on the dark planet Geidi Prime. Like their nemesis the Atreides, they are one of the Great Houses, which together with the Emperor and the Spacing Guild form the CHOAM (Combine Honnete Ober Advancer Mercantiles) corporation. CHOAM controls the harvesting of Spice on Arrakis and its distribution throughout the universe.

The Baron is assisted in his ruthless scheming ways by his two nephews, Feyd and his brother Rabban. All three were terrors in their own way.

Treacherous and unprincipled, the Baron is a glutton with a voracious appetite for pleasure and a strong hatred for the Atreides.

Feyd Harkonnen was raised by the Baron and was well-schooled in Harkonnen ruthlessness. He honed his fighting techniques by killing slaves who never really had a fair chance.

The Fremen name for Rabban is Mudir Nahya, which translates as

Feyd

"Demon Ruler." The Harkonnens mercilessly subjugated the Fremen during their rule on Arrakis, and Rabban was the Baron's regent there.

Ian McNeice had big shoes to fill as Baron Harkonnen. "I'm fairly big myself," the actor admits, "but they padded me out on top of that." In describing the character he plays McNeice stated, "I think the Baron is one of those delicious Machiavellian characters that is tremendous fun for an actor. I mean he's basically a hedonist. He gorges on everything he sees. His hatred of the House Atreides is also foremost in his mind. In the sequence where Duke Leto dies, the Baron delivers a three-and-a-half page tirade. William [Hurt] sat in a chair opposite me playing a drugged Duke Leto and I basically spattered him with venom for twelve hours. I think he just had one word at the end of it, that's all. I had to thank him for being so patient.

"But I knew that if all I did was go down the Baron's road of anger and play this one note it could get awfully boring. I managed to find a tremendous amount of humor in the Baron as well and bring that out."

Ian McNeice was in London working on a David Copperfield TV

Rabban

mini-series when his agent told him that the producers of "Frank Herbert's Dune" were interested in talking to him.

"I remembered the movie, and I was very excited because I knew the character very well. The producers and director were interested in a screen test. Luckily the cameraman on the show at the time said he'd help me do something, so we did a screen test with a digital video cam-

Rabban

era. I was wearing a 'bald' cap at the time. I thought it would be fun to do something with this so, having read one of the nastier pieces for the part, I tore the skull cap off and revealed this shock of hair underneath. I subsequently heard from John Harrison that they were completely astounded. I think it helped me land the role."

McNeice knew ahead of time that one of the unusual character traits of the Baron was that he didn't walk, but instead floated above the ground via anti-gravity devices crafted to support his enormous bulk. The special effects crew rigged up a crane to float the actor just slightly above the floor, and when necessary in extreme circumstances, up to fifteen feet in the air.

In describing the device, McNeice recalled, "They'd built this extension onto a camera crane which was rather comfortable, like a tractor seat. I would sit on this and they could take me and put me up high or move me around. But when it looked as though I was sitting rather than standing, they had to make an adjustment. The device then turned into something rather like a vicious metal bicycle seat, which made my legs go down either side more in a straight line, and with the long costume

Baron Harkonnen

you couldn't tell how I was supported. But it was incredibly painful. I'm quite a large man, so the whole weight went on to this metal bicycle seat. They did put a bit of foam under there near the end, but I remember that it became a living nightmare.

"I really had to put up with it because I knew that in order to take me down it would take some time to get me up again. So there were times when I just had to grit my teeth and bear it. They were very good about how much they used it and they knew that when I went into it they'd have to move quite quickly, and luckily they used stunt men to do the rehearsals, so I'd get on it and we'd film pretty quick.

"It became an amazing thing and you could travel quite fast in it and go up quite high in it. Vittorio Storaro, who is a god of a cinematographer, was very enthusiastic. It became rather a good process of director, actor and cinematographer working as a team, as opposed to 'We're going to do this next.' What was amazing was that I actually didn't have to hit a mark myself or walk for seven weeks and at the end of it, there was this one Czech grip who'd done all the work in pushing me around and finding the marks, and on my final day I got a trolley with several

Far left: Baron Harkonnen; far right: Piter Devries (*Jan Unger*)

cases of his favorite beer, which was rolled out at the end, and I said to him, 'George, all you have to do now is push that home.' "

One of his costars in "Frank Herbert's Dune" is actress Saskia Reeves, who Ian McNeice met while she was still attending drama school in London, England.

"I actually directed her in a couple of shows," McNeice recalled. "One was *Measure For Measure* and I knew then that she had tremendous talent. She very sweetly looks back at this point and says, 'You're the only one that ever said anything nice about my work.' After she left drama school she didn't stop. She did TV movie after movie and really hasn't stopped since." Although they both feature largely in the story, they actually only have one scene together. "There's a scene where she's strapped down and she's in front of me and I have another tirade. I seem to be doing it all the time. "

Ian's film and television credits stretch back some twenty years. They start in England and include such productions as *The Life And Adventures of Nicholas Nickleby* (1981), *Top Secret!* (1984), *84 Charing Cross Road* (1986), *Edge of Darkness* (1986), *Cry Freedom* (1987), *Valmont* (1989), *Around The World In 80 Days* (1989 TV mini-series), *The Russia House* (1990), *Year Of The Comet* (1992), *The Wimbledon Poisoner* (1994 TV mini-series), *Funny Bones* (1995), *The Englishman Who Went Up A Hill But Came Down A Mountain* (1995), *Ace Ventura: When Nature Calls* (1995), *A*

Baron Harkonnen

Life Less Ordinary (1997), *A Christmas Carol* (1999), and *Longitude* (2000, a TV mini-series).

In "Frank Herbert's Dune," Feyd Harkonnen is played by Matt Keeslar. In the context of the story, the Bene Gesserit had intended Jessica Atreides to have a daughter by Duke Leto, and this daughter was destined to marry Feyd. When Jessica defied the Bene Gesserit by giving the Duke a son, Paul and Feyd were set on a collision course from which only one would ultimately emerge.

Keeslar is comfortable playing Feyd, but he doesn't diminish the dangerous side of the character he portrays.

"The thing about Feyd is that he's the ultimate sociopath," the actor readily admits. "He doesn't have any remorse about killing. He lives for excitement. He lives for the moment. In the mini-series he celebrates his one hundredth kill of a slave . . . you almost think of him as some sort of very spoiled professional athlete. He trains all the time, and part of his training is this killing that he does which is a rite of passage for Harkonnen boys."

Above and below: Feyd and Baron Harkonnen

Piter Devries and Lady Jessica

Keeslar was born in Grand Rapids, Michigan in 1972. After receiving training at Julliard, he began appearing in films in 1994 in *Safe Passage*, *Renaissance Man* and *Quiz Show*. These were followed by a TV production of *A Streetcar Named Desire* (1995), *Waiting For Guffman* (1996), *Mr. Magoo* (1997), *The Last Days of Disco* (1998), *Durango* (1999), and in the year 2000 was *Urbania*, *Psycho Beach Party* and *Scream 3*.

Above: Feyd; below: Feyd and Paul Atreides

A Harkonnen soldier

Emperor Shaddam IV and Reverend Mother Mohiam

THE EMPEROR

T he Emperor, Shaddam IV resides in his imperial seat on the planet Kaitain, guarded by crack troops known as the Sardaukar. The Emperor is a controlling partner in CHOAM. In "Frank Herbert's Dune," he orders Duke Leto to relocate the House Atreides to Arrakis and take over the production of Spice. Duke Leto has no choice but to comply.

Emperor Shaddam IV is played by Italian film star Giancarlo Giannini. Born in La Spezoa, Italy in 1942, he has appeared in numerous European motion pictures and came to prominence with American audiences in Lina Wertmüller's *Swept Away* (1975). He has also appeared in Sidney Sheldon's *Bloodline* (1979), as well as *American Dreamer* (1984), *New York Stories* (1989), *Once Upon A Crime* (1992), *Jacob: A TNT Bible Story* (1994), *A Walk In The Clouds* (1995), *Mimic* (1997), and others.

"Giancarlo was a favorite actor of both John [Harrison] and myself for many years," said executive producer Mitchell Galin. "When we explored whether or not he was available for the role, we were excited to learn that he knew the material well and wanted to partake in the project right away."

The Emperor's daughter is Princess Irulan. While Frank Herbert made

Emperor Shaddam IV

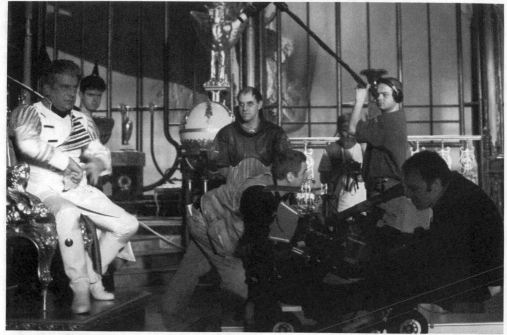

Preparing for a scene

her the narrator in his first *Dune* novel, in the mini-series she steps forward as a character who participates in events as they occur. She is sent to Arrakis, after Duke Leto is sent to take over, as a gesture of the Emperor's good will. This is when she and Paul first meet.

"Princess Irulan is very intelligent, fiery and independent, and coquettish when she needs to be, but not for her own personal gain, because she's Bene Gesserit trained," explains actress Julie Cox, who plays her. "She has a very childlike quality, but great maturity and wisdom, and she probably would be a much better emperor than her father. But she's a woman and the Emperor was waiting for a son. She very much loves her father but is disappointed in him for treating her as 'just a girl.' She has her own designs and aspirations to become a leader. But because she doesn't have the nerve to do that yet, she becomes a great scholar.

"She meets Paul quite early on in the story and there's an immediate connection. They're very similar and come from similar backgrounds. Similar temperaments. And if circumstances were different they probably would have been a great couple.

"She's very much aware of the moral issues behind the conflicts that are going on and the way her father is dealing with them. It makes her fight to find out what's really going on. She is driven by a sense of good and a desire to find the truth behind things."

Julie Cox is a young actress whose film work dates back to 1993

Emperor Shaddam IV

when she appeared in Franz Kafka's *It's A Wonderful Life*. She also played the child-like empress in *The Never Ending Story III* (1994), as well as having roles in *Danielle Steel's Zoya* (1995), *Death Machine* (1995), *Danielle Steel's The Ring* (1996), *Princess In Love* (1996, in which she played Princess Diana), the 1997 TV mini-series *20,000 Leagues Under The Sea*, and the 1999 TV movie of *The Scarlet Pimpernel*. "Frank Herbert's Dune" is her first epic adventure. Landing the role in "Frank Herbert's Dune" was particularly fortuitous since she was already very familiar with the novel itself.

"My agent in London had already cast a couple of people in this and

A palace guard

she mentioned it to me and didn't realize that I was already a big fan of the book," the actress recalled. "I said, 'Absolutely, yes!' In the book my character is the narrator, but in the mini-series she plays a much more active role. I like the way John [Harrison] adapted it very much, he made it stronger."

Since Irulan is an active participant in the story of "Frank Herbert's Dune," the love triangle involving Paul Atredies and the Freman woman Chani is more pronounced, as is the parallel between the love shared by Jessica and Duke Leto.

Julie observed that, "I think there's a mutual respect between Jessica and Irulan. They understand each other because they both had to do things for the better of people other than themselves. Jessica made a personal sacrifice because of her love for the Duke by producing a son instead of a daughter. Near the end of the story Irulan suggests that to end the war that is tearing everything apart, she and Paul Atreides should marry. Irulan knows there is no future for herself, that there's no love for her in this marriage, yet because of the greater issues it seems the right decision."

Cox was particularly gratified that the cinematographer was Vittorio Storaro, which insured that it would be above average in look as well as execution. "When I found out that Vittorio was the cinematographer, it was a bit of a shock and it took awhile to sink in because I'm just a big fan of his. But when I actually watched how he approached his work,

Princess Irulan

Princess Irulan

and the amount of energy and thought he put into it, my respect for him shot up even more. He's a very patient, gentle man."

The actress is impressed by not just the craftsmanship of the film-makers, but by her co-workers as well.

"One of the things that appealed to me the most was the quality of the cast. And when you're working on something of this nature, you have to bring a lot of levels behind the character; it makes the environment real. The dialogue is shared with the costumes, and the sets—all part of one package. John said, when he and I discussed my part, that the story is the real hero. There's been a wonderful generosity from the cast for what we do. There's a wonderful level of talent here and we're all playing a part of the puzzle."

Paul Atreides and Princess Irulan

Stilgar

Fremen

THE FREMEN

Fremen are the native inhabitants of Arrakis. Mysterious and secretive, they know more than they seem to and in fact help contribute to the life cycle of the gigantic sandworms and the method by which the worms produce Spice. The Fremen are a loosely ordered group of 'tribes' who are united by common goals and heritage. While they seem to be a patriarchal society, they are nonetheless strongly influenced by the "wise women" called Reverend Mothers and the beliefs of the Bene Gesserit which have been sown on their world.

Because water on Arrakis is so scarce, the Fremen have developed a method of recycling their personal water in what are called "Stillsuits." A Stillsuit is made from a micro-sandwich fabric, which filters bodily wastes and heat dissipation and reclaims their moisture in catchpockets.

Three Fremen

The wearer can then access the water in the catchpockets via a straw-like tube. The Fremen also use a Stilltent when they are outside the Sietch (the cave warrens where the Fremen communities live). The Stilltent is made of the same micro-sandwich fabric as the Stillsuit, and is designed to reclaim the moisture from the air exhaled by those who are within the Stilltent.

In keeping with his desire to set the Fremen apart from the other inhabitants of Dune, director John Harrison conceived of the notion that the Fremen would probably pass down cultural information and moral teachings to their children in the form of stories, and that some of these stories could be related in puppet shows. To accomplish this he turned to Petr and Matej Forman, twin brothers who are master puppeteers in the Czech Republic. They still carve their own puppets, just as the master puppeteers of old did. Petr and Matej Forman (sons of Oscar winning director Milos Forman) appear on screen as Fremen bards, using puppet shows to teach history and morality to Fremen children.

The lives of the Fremen were first changed by the arrival of the planetary ecologist, Pardot Kynes, and then again by the arrival of the House Atreides and Paul Atreides, the "Mah'di"—the messiah. Pardot Kynes became the leader of the Fremen and his leadership was succeeded by his son, Liet-Kynes. Liet-Kynes worked with the Fremen in their goal to make Arrakis a paradise at some future time by creating an ecosystem

Above: Fremen
puppeteers telling a
story to children;
right: A Fremen
puppet

Chani and Paul Atreides

that contained water. Although he was the Fremen leader, Liet-Kynes did not interfere with the leadership of the individual tribes and allowed the "Naibs" (Fremen word for "Chief") of each tribe to lead. His daughter Chani is the Fremen woman who becomes Paul Atreides' true love.

When Paul and Jessica Atreides escape to the desert, they only survive because they are taken in by the Fremen tribe from Sietch Tabr, which is led by Stilgar. Stilgar plays a very important role in "Frank Herbert's Dune" because he becomes Paul's mentor and teaches him the

A Fremen ceremony

Stilgar

A Fremen warrior

ways of the desert. He takes up where Duke Leto left off in helping Paul to become a man and helps guide him towards his destiny. Stilgar is played by German film star, Uwe Ochsenknecht. Born January 7, 1956 in Mannheim, Germany, among his many acting credits is *Das Boot* (*The*

Above: Chani and Paul Atreides; below: a Fremen ambush

Chani

Boat) the 1980 film directed by Wolfgang Peterson. In 1986 he won the Film Strip in Gold Award for the film *Manner* (1985) and in 1998 was nominated for the Film Strip in Gold Award for the film *Weihnachtsfieber*.

The role of Chani is played by Barbora Kodetova. Her previous film roles include *The Dance Master* (1995), *Rivers of Babylon* (1998) and the Swedish film *The Stronger* (1999). "I'm a theater actress, primarily for the Prague theater. I've played in some films and TV shows on Czech television. But, until this mini-series I've never had experience with a big production from America.

In describing her character, she discusses how Chani matures from a girl into a woman over the course of the story. "She's a Fremen girl. She's a very nice person. Strong. The relationship between Chani and Paul starts with love. She is a young girl and he is a young guy, and they fall in love in a romantic way. Then their life changes when the war comes. Their relationship changes. They go through very bad things

Chani prepares to get the Water of Life from a sandworm.

Lady Jessica prepares for the Water of Life ceremony.

together. In the end in order to end the war, she's strong enough to say, 'There are times when it's necessary to share the one you love with things greater than both of you. You have to marry Princess Irulan. I will be here for you for your life, but it's important for you and for all of us.' "

Among the many Fremen ceremonies portrayed in "Frank Herbert's Dune," one of the most sacred involves the "Water of Life." The Water of Life is the liquid a sandworm vomits at the moment of its death from drowning. During the Water of Life ceremony in the miniseries, Jessica Atreides must drink this poisonous liquid and use her Bene Gesserit abilities to change it from poison to water. If she is successful in transforming the water and lives, she will reach a higher state of awareness and become a Reverend Mother. She undergoes this ceremony while pregnant with Paul's sister, Alia. The effect on the unborn Alia proves to have many consequences later in the *Dune* saga.

Reverend Mother Mohiam

Reverend Mother Mohiam and Bene Gesserit attendant

BENE GESSERIT

The Bene Gesserit was the first mental-physical training school established (primarily for female students) after the Butlerian Jihad. This war marked an important turning point in history because it ultimately resulted in the outlawing of thinking machines and the making of a machine that worked like a human mind. Thus developing the human mind became pre-eminent, particularly among certain factions who could use this to their particular advantage. The Bene Gesserit have learned to detect patterns in history and know events before they happen. Both Jessica Atreides and Reverend Mother Mohiam knew that Duke Leto was doomed, and that there was nothing they could do to prevent it. This knowledge of the future can enable more insightful decisions to be made, but they do not use their abilities to alter the inevitable—at least that is what they are taught. However, the sisterhood

Lady Jessica and Stilgar

works to manipulate events and uses subtlety and subterfuge to achieve its goals.

This ancient sisterhood spread to all the known worlds in the universe, sowing implant legends through the "Missionaria Protectiva." Thus when a member of the order came to a world which may have otherwise had little contact or commerce with the Imperium, there were legends in place which a member of the Bene Gesserit could capitalize on to gain influence in what would otherwise be an alien culture. The Lady Jessica Atreides quickly took advantage of this upon her arrival on Arrakis.

Before she became the concubine of Duke Leto, Jessica Atreides was instructed by the sisterhood that as a Bene Gesserit she existed to serve the sisterhood. When Jessica was chosen by the Duke, this fit perfectly into their plans to manipulate the bloodlines of both House Atreides and House Harkonnen and bring about a unification of the two Houses. They foresaw this by having Jessica give the Duke a daughter to marry the male Harkonnen heir. But Jessica defied her teachings for the love of her Duke. When she chose instead to give the Duke the son he desired, events were altered dramatically. This wild card proved to be greater than any-

Paul Atreides and Reverend Mother Mohiam

Reverend Mother Ramallo

thing the sisterhood had foreseen because Paul Atreides became the *Kwisatz Haderach*, which means "Shortening of the Way." This is the label applied by the Bene Gesserit to the unknown for which they sought a genetic solution: a male Bene Gesserit whose organic mental powers would bridge space and time. While they suspected that Paul Atreides could in fact be this *Kwisatz Haderach*, they were afraid to believe that he was. If it were true, then it would mean that he would be beyond the reach of their control and a threat to the foundation of their power.

Lady Jessica and grandson Leto

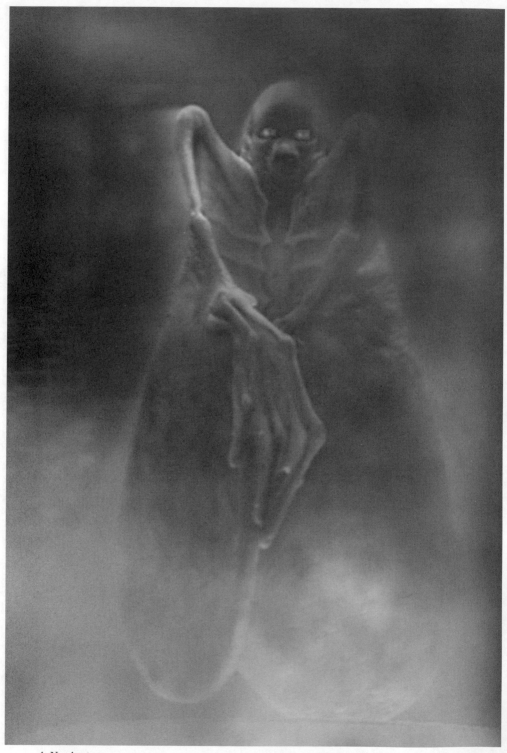

A Navigator

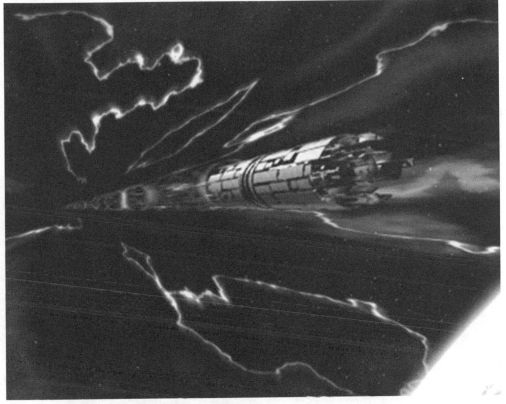

A Heighliner spaceship folding space

THE SPACING GUILD

The Navigators of the Spacing Guild are the most mysterious players in the *Dune* saga. The Guild was the second mental-physical training school established after the Butlerian Jihad. (The Bene Gesserit was the first.) The Guild managed to use Spice to learn how to manipulate space and time and achieve faster-than-light travel. As a result, the genetically manipulated Guild Navigators were able to step in and do what computers had done, before they were outlawed. They are the only ones who have this ability and therefore control interstellar space travel. It is a secret they jealously guard and use to maintain an important position of power in the Imperium. When contracted to move a ship a vast distance through space in days (where other methods would take years), the travelers they transport are sealed in their vessel and never even see the Guild Navigator that controls their vessel.

Spice, which is found only on Arrakis, is vital to the Guild's mastery of space. Spice has qualities vital to unleashing certain mental abilities

A Spacing Guild Representative

and affects the space-time awareness center in the brain. One can only assume the vast quantities of Spice that are ingested by Guild Navigators to perceive space-time in hyperspace in order to move interstellar ships vast distances in short periods of time. Its use in space travel is what makes the Spice such a vital, sought-after organic compound of incredible valuable.

In Frank Herbert's novel *Dune*, the Spacing Guild is mentioned but they remain a mysterious off-stage presence. In the book, when the House Atreides is transported from Caladan to Arrakis, it occurs between chapters. This would not have been as effective on screen. What follows are four pages of the visual effects storyboard from the mini-series, which demonstrates how a Guild Navigator (portrayed as being an alien-looking being with some general human characteristics) navigates a Heighliner between the stars. It's a scene not found in the novel.

DUNE / Folding Space / Scs 9 ,11, 12 / p. 4 of 7

...a grotesque, web-footed creature emerges...

FS-1041 (continued)

...rising up out of the carriage...

FS-1041 (continued)

...into the column of gas. The Navigator.

FS-1042

FS-1043

FS-1043 (continued)

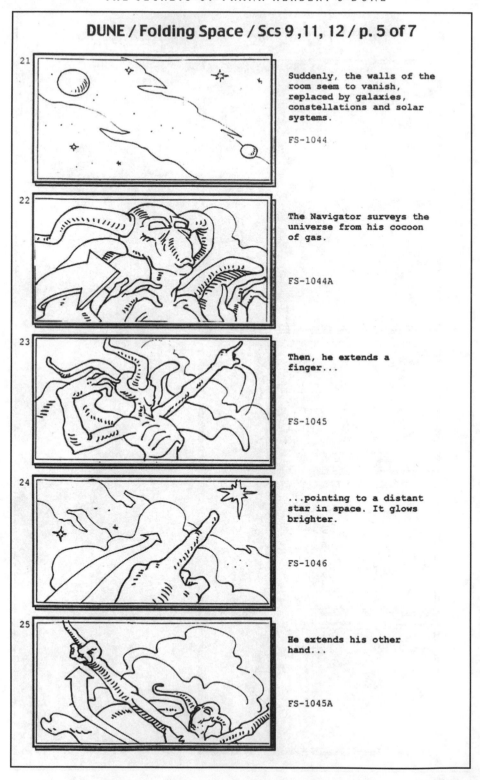

DUNE / Folding Space / Scs 9 ,11, 12 / p. 5 of 7

21 — Suddenly, the walls of the room seem to vanish, replaced by galaxies, constellations and solar systems.

FS-1044

22 — The Navigator surveys the universe from his cocoon of gas.

FS-1044A

23 — Then, he extends a finger...

FS-1045

24 — ...pointing to a distant star in space. It glows brighter.

FS-1046

25 — He extends his other hand...

FS-1045A

DUNE / Folding Space / Scs 9 ,11, 12 / p. 6 of 7

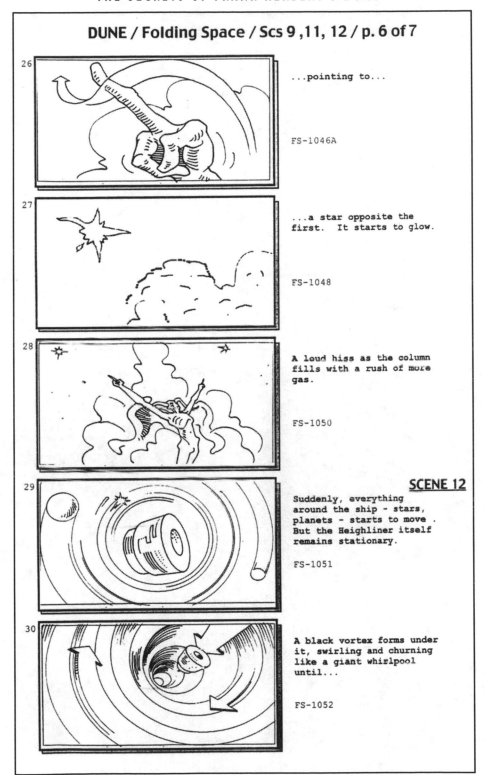

26

...pointing to...

FS-1046A

27

...a star opposite the first. It starts to glow.

FS-1048

28

A loud hiss as the column fills with a rush of more gas.

FS-1050

29

SCENE 12

Suddenly, everything around the ship - stars, planets - starts to move . But the Heighliner itself remains stationary.

FS-1051

30

A black vortex forms under it, swirling and churning like a giant whirlpool until...

FS-1052

DUNE / Folding Space / Scs 9 ,11, 12 / p. 7 of 7

31

...the Heighliner drops down into it, and the void literally folds in around it.

FS-1052 (continued)

32

And suddenly, the blur is gone and the stars return. The Heighliner has vanished...

FS-1054

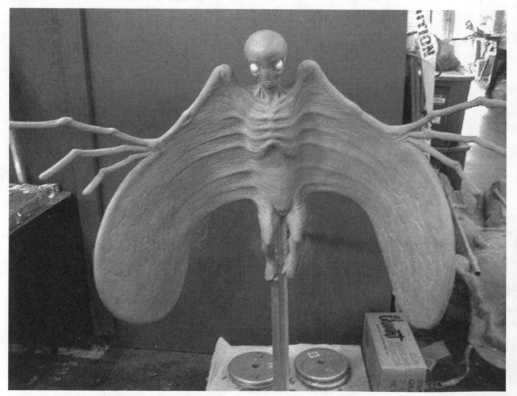

A Navigator puppet

PRODUCTION

Left: Miljen "Kreka" Kljakovic; middle: John Harrison

PRODUCTION DESIGNER MILJEN "KREKA" KLJAKOVIC

The Production Designer on "Frank Herbert's Dune" is Miljen Kljakovic, better known as "Kreka."

"In August of 1999, Kreka joined me in Los Angeles," said director John Harrison. "We sat outside in the hot California sun for two weeks thinking about life on Dune, what kind of place it would be, how people would survive there. What would they eat? What kind of tools did they use? Herbert created this wonderfully complex universe of the ancient and the futuristic, of the feudal and the corporate. How were we going to manifest such a complicated vision?

"Every day we would talk and speculate. Kreka would draw and sketch until we finally had a workable scheme for the entire production. Kaitain where the Emperor lives, is very art nouveau, very elegant with lots of golds and purples. The planet Geidi Prime where the Harkonnen live has red as its predominant color and is also defined by the jagged angles of its architecture that suggest one might actually hurt oneself brushing up against it. Arrakis, or Dune, is a desert world, of course. The palace in the city of Arrakeen is this elegant Moroccan-style palace which has stood for centuries in the middle of nowhere. The way Kreka designed it, you feel that it is an ancient place. Kreka crafted a very stylized look for each of the planets."

Two production sketches by Kreka

SIETCH TABR - DUNE
DIRECTOR JOHN HARRISON
PRODUCTION MILJEU- KREKA-KLJAKOVIĆ
DESIGNER

A Space Guild representative in the Emperor's library

Kreka also worked closely with cinematographer Vittorio Storaro to coordinate and compliment in the sets the thematic color schemes Vittorio would be using for the lighting. The alien realms of the miniseries allowed Kreka to use his imagination to its fullest when it came to designing the sets. He also designed something different for each of the palaces.

"When you say a palace you usually think about big, huge columns and very ornamental lighting," he said. "But for this mini-series I wanted to do something really strange. So in the palace on Arrakis, the columns contain lights inside a special glass because I didn't want to put the usual chandeliers or other lights."

He takes pride in the level of workmanship his crew displayed on the mini-series. Pointing to a wall, he said, "This wall is plaster, but when the painters finish their job it will be very detailed and beautiful. It will look like a palace, not a set."

Actress Julie Cox (who plays Princess Irulan) experienced Kreka's imaginative realm of "Frank Herbert's Dune" from the inside.

"As an actress, you're always imagining places like this," she said. "Working on sets this beautiful, is inspiring. It can only make you feel

A set under construction

like you are that character, and you can believe that this is where you live. This is who I am."

Kreka's credits include *Time of the Gypsies* (1989), *Delicatesse* (1991), *Arizona Dream* (1993), *Underground* (1995), *Rasputine* (1996), *The Brave* (1997) and *Species II* (1998).

John Harrison and Theodor Pistek

THE COSTUME DESIGNS OF THEODOR PISTEK
Comments by John Harrison

"**F**rank Herbert's Dune" is not off the rack in any way, shape or form. The various factions are very well defined in Frank Herbert's book. I wanted to make sure that in our mini-series each one of those 'tribes', if you will, had a distinct look and identifiable style that would immediately tell an audience, "I'm with the Imperial family." Or "I'm with the Atreides family." Each very highly stylized. Theodor Pistek's wardrobe design by itself tells you something about each of the characters.

Pistek is a Czech national treasure. He's one of the country's premiere artists. He's designed costumes for feature motion pictures as well as hundreds of stage presentations; in fact he won an Academy Award for his costume design for *Amadeus*.

Interestingly, he had never designed for a science fiction movie, and had actually avoided it. When we first met, he was reluctant to work on "Frank Herbert's Dune." His prior work has been mostly period drama, like *Amadeus*. He really didn't want to create the kind of futuristic look that we've all become accustomed to in science fiction. I wooed him by saying that this mini-series was more of a period piece than a futuristic

Fremen musicians

drama. Even though it's set twenty-three thousand years in the future, the intergalactic society has reverted to an almost medieval type of civilization. We therefore wanted to avoid the tight-fitting spandex or the clean shapeless wardrobe that we see so often associated with current sci-fi. To some degree, I wanted our costume designs to be more retro.

Pistek and I sat down and started talking about the different styles that I wanted. I gave him very broad ideas. I'd give him examples; metaphors for what I would think the individual family or tribe would be like. And in a global sense, I'd talk about the feudal nature of one society in the story as opposed to the high tech characteristics of another. Pistek would then go off and draw. The first set of designs that he

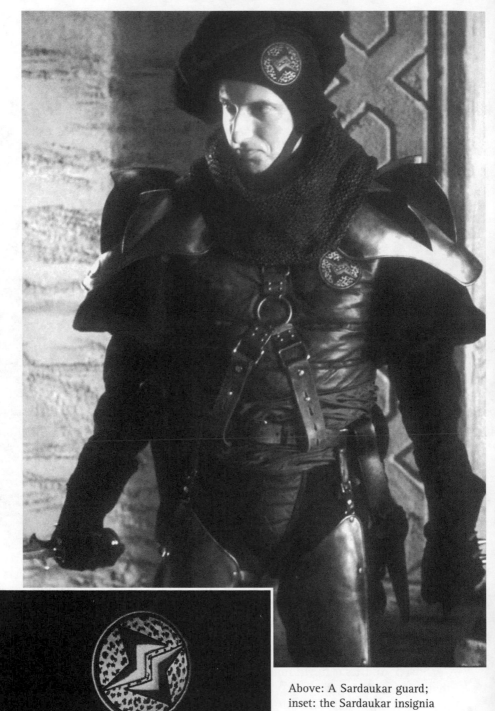

Above: A Sardaukar guard;
inset: the Sardaukar insignia

Left: A senior advisor to the Emperor; right: A Sardaukar guard

showed me were almost dead on for so many characters. In fact I would venture to say that the first set of drawings that he did are all in the miniseries.

After Vittorio Storaro arrived we discussed Pistek's designs with color in mind because Storaro is incredibly sophisticated in his view of the use of color as a psychological tool. With Pistek's designs and Vittorio's suggestions for color, we came up with what I think are really memorable looks for each family. For example, we decided that the Imperial family would resonate in gold and violet, and not-quite blues. The Imperial wardrobes are very ornate and ornamental. To create an intimidating look for the Emperor's Sardaukar guards, Pistek turned to

Top, left to right: Feyd, Emperor Shaddam IV and Princess Irulan; bottom: Chani

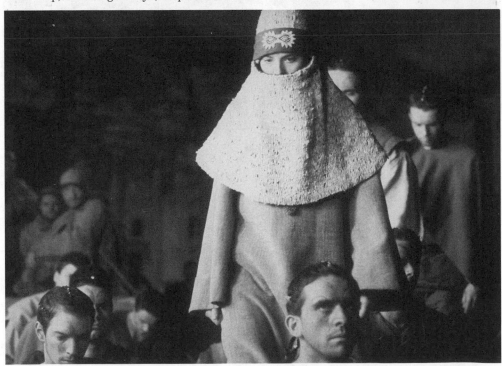

Duke Leto Atreides (*William Hurt*)

Lady Jessica (*Saskia Reeves*)

Above: Paul Atreides (*Alec Newman*)
Below: Feyd Harkonnen (*Matt Keeslar*)

Chani (*Barbora Kodetova*)

Princess Irulan (*Julie Cox*)

Above: Princess Irulan and Paul Atreides
Below: Chani and Paul

Emperor Shaddam IV
(*Giancarlo Giannini*)

Stilgar (*Uwe Ochsenknecht*)

Above Left: Guild Agent (*Phil Lenkowsky*)
Above Right: Baron Harkonnen (*Ian McNeice*)
Below: Princess Irulan (*Julie Cox*) presented to the court at the
Arrakeen Palace by Duke Leto (*William Hurt*).

Above: Thufir Hawat (*Jan Vlasak*)

Below: Dr. Kynes (*Karel Dobry*)

Above and below: Paul Atreides' sister, Alia (*Laura Burton*), a prisoner in the Emperor's palace

Above: The Emperor receives bad news as Guild Agent, Count Fenring (*Miroslav Taborsky*) and Bene Gesserit Reverend Mother Mohiam (*Zuzana Geislerova*) watch.
Below Left: Rabban (*Laszlo Imre Kish*) and Feyd Harkonnen (*Matt Keeslar*).

Above, Left to Right: Jamis, Stilgar, Lady Jessica and Chani in Sietch Tabr. Below: Shooting a Fremen scene on one of the Arrakis desert sets.

Above: Duke Leto's banquet at Arrakeen Palace. Below: The Fremen attack the Harkonnen who have seized Arrakeen Palace.

Above: Actors fleeing a doomed Harvester, shot against a blue screen. Below: Paul Atreides about to ride a worm.

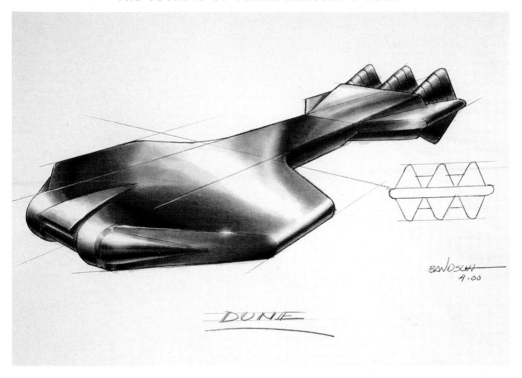

Above and Below: Production sketches of two flying vehicles by Netter Digital..

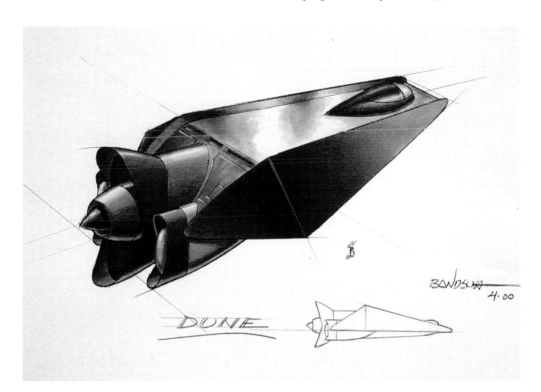

The Harkonnen Palace on the planet Geidi Prime.

Pistek's design for one of Lady Jessica's gowns

ancient Japanese Samurai warrior garb for inspiration. Spiked, metal-plated body armor complemented the Far Eastern-style cut and jet black cloth. "I feel like a human Humvee," one Sardaukar soldier told us.

The Atreides wardrobes are very functional and very chameleon-like. The earth tones of the planet Dune were our inspiration for the

Top: Pistek's butterfly gown for Princess Irulan; bottom left: House Atreides insignia; bottom right: Harkonnen soldier insignias

Fremen. I always had a very industrial, almost Blake-ian vision of what the Harkonnen world was like. So, Pistek designed all of the Harkonnen costumes with a lot of edges and red tones, which make for a very uncomfortable feeling.

One of the biggest problems that we had was the design of the

One of Pistek's finished costumes

Top: An example of one of the elaborate hats designed by Pistek; bottom: one of Pistek's many dresses for Princess Irulan

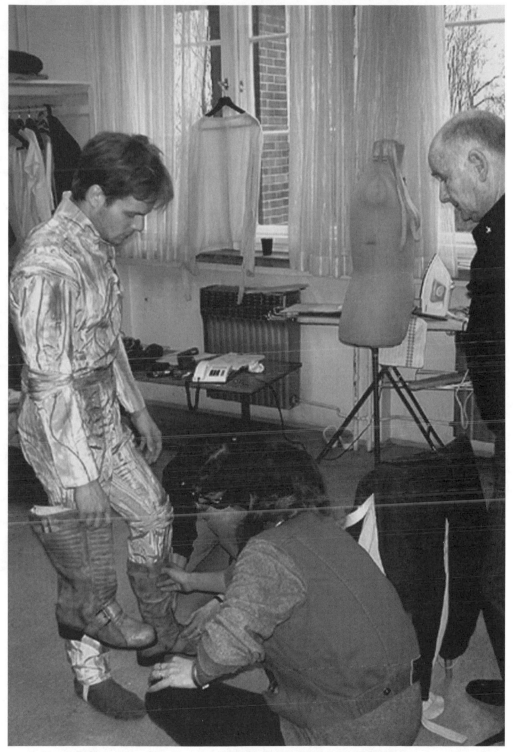

Pistek (left) watches Alec Newman (right) getting fitted into a Stillsuit

Lady Jessica and Alia (*Laura Burton*)

Stillsuits that the Fremen use to recycle the wearer's bodily fluids. We had to find a way to adapt what Herbert described to fit in with the overall Fremen thematic and at the same time they had to appear practical. I think we came up with something that is very effective.

Each principal character had multiple wardrobes in addition to costumes for the attendants, family, guards, soldiers and extras that were all around every one of those individuals. For example, the Emperor had five costumes. Princess Irulan had half a dozen. The Fremen in contrast, had only the same outfit all the time, because it was their desert wear, with the exception of their Stillsuit. Duke Leto had several different wardrobes. Because Paul is Atreides, then he becomes Fremen, and then becomes the Emperor, he had a good half a dozen or more wardrobe changes. Baron Harkonnen had six. Then there were all the costumes for minor characters like a Water Master with the Fremen, or a smuggler with Gurney Halleck out in the desert, or an Atreides lieutenant, or a Harkonnen soldier. There were differences between the Imperial Guards and the Sardaukar mercenaries.

In the end, Pistek and his team created hundreds of original costumes, all changing in a recognizable pattern with the flow of the story. At times, this visual feast is almost overwhelming, as in the final act of the drama where every major character is represented during the final confrontation between Paul Atreides and the Emperor. But the way Pistek's designs integrate themselves into the completed look of this production is both masterful and seamless.

Matt Keeslar who plays Feyd Harkonnen said, "You can tell that Theodor Pistek wants to fully realize each of the characters within their costumes, and each of the people in the movie. Even if they're only extras who have one line, their costumes have been specifically tailored to fit them as part of his vision. It's pretty exceptional. I've never really worked with a designer who was that determined to be that specific."

Paul Atreides and his court

Paul

One of Pistek's many costume designs for Paul Atreides

Chani in her official court attire

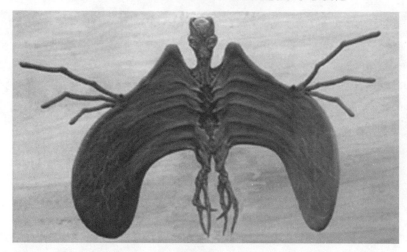

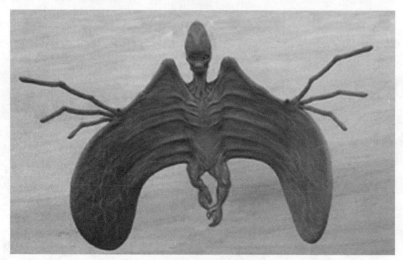

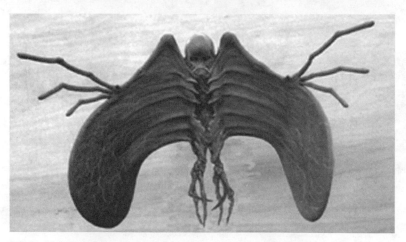

Three designs for the Guild Navigator

A Guild Navigator puppet

THE MECHANICAL EFFECTS

GREG NICOTERO: KNB FX GROUP

Sandworms and The Guild Navigator

The flesh and blood of KNB Effects Group is Robert Kurtzman, Greg Nicotero and Howard Berger. The company was formed in 1988 and has major credits on many feature films including: *Spawn, Wishmaster, From Dusk 'Til Dawn, Army Of Darkness, Dances With Wolves, Misery, Eraser* (where they did the alligators), and *The Green Mile* (the execution scene).

On "Frank Herbert's Dune" the KNB Effects Group was responsible for all of the puppet creature effects, including the Guild Navigator and the non-CGI sandworms.

Greg Nicotero says, "I have a long history with Richard [Rubinstein] and John [Harrison] because I worked on *Day of the Dead* in 1985, where Richard was the producer and John was the first A. D. When John got his feature directorial debut from Richard and Paramount on *Tales From The Darkside: The Movie*, he hired KNB to do the effects.

The sandworm operating crew; note the levers and cables going into the water

"We spent a lot of time sitting with John and going through the script and fleshing out designs for the Guild Navigator and sandworms. We probably did thirty different Navigator designs and tons of worm designs, not only artwork but three-dimensional sculptures, as well.

"One of the difficulties we faced was that once we got the 'green light' and started working on the designs, John left for Prague. So we really didn't have access to him because he was half a world away, as was Kreka, the production designer.

Another challenge facing KNB was in the construction of the stunted adult worm puppet. The scene in which it was being shot required that the puppet be in waist deep water with several actors. This meant that the puppet could not be electrical, so KNB created a fully mechanical puppet with gears, cables, and levers that was operated by five offstage puppeteers.

"The stunted adult worm was a tricky puppet to make because it had to be able to work underwater as well as out of water. Further complicating matters was that we had to send videotape to Prague showing what we were making in order to be certain that it was exactly what John wanted in terms of what it could do. When the sequence began, John wanted to see the worm moving just a little bit under the water before two Fremen enter and grab it. Chani then wades in and sticks a bag over the worm's mouth and the sandworm vomits 'The Water of Life'

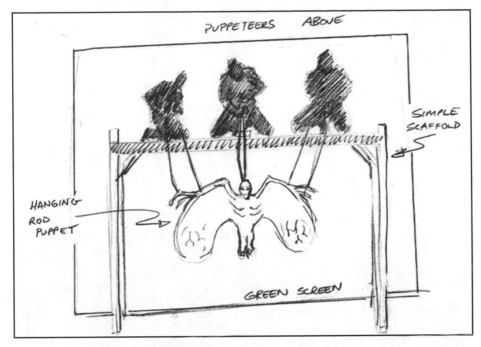

Top: A sketch of the Guild Navigator puppet and puppet masters;
Bottom: A section of the sandworm skin; note visual effects "green screen" far left

A Guild Navigator puppet

into the bag. In addition to having to move realistically underwater, once the two actors grabbed it, the worm had to start thrashing around like it was trying to escape, and finally it had to open its mouth and vomit! It was a tremendous challenge for us. We ended up only spending a day and a half shooting all the puppet scenes in Prague, which is really amazing if you think about how complex it is to shoot effects using puppets. That was actually the only time that we were physically on location with the rest of the crew.

"The other worm puppets were for the different physical actions of the worms, including moving underneath the sand, the heads bursting out of the sand, and the heads going back under the sand. All of the puppets actually had skins made from foam latex, but the internal mechanisms were tubes that were segmented."

Everything took time to make. "The stunted worms took two and a half months to make. The Guild Navigator about a month and a half, and the large worms took about four months.

"We also made a full size section of the large worm for the actors to stand on in front of a blue screen so that they could composite in the background later on. It had the wormskin hard plates and little soft fleshy areas so that the Fremen could throw their grappling hooks up and hook onto it."

Paul Atreides and Fremen on a sandworm

KNB did the rest of its work on "Frank Herbert's Dune" at their Los Angeles studio where they shot the other worm puppets and the Guild Navigator.

Referring to the navigator Greg said, "It was really a challenge to create this unique looking humanoid character. It has these super-evolved lobes that almost looked like wings, but really were enlarged lungs because it had been living in the Spice gas for such a long period of time and had evolved away from human form."

Three views of a
sandworm showing
the scale to a
Harvester and
Paul Atreides

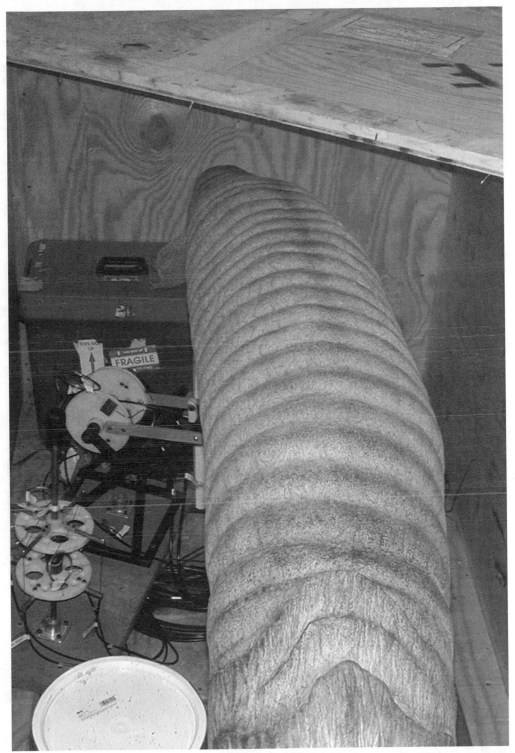

The small adult sandworm puppet in its shipping crate

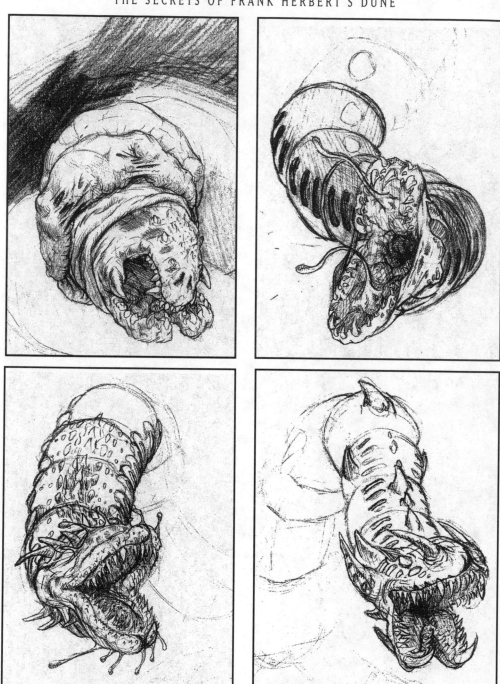

Four preliminary sandworm sketches

Riding a sandworm

Ernest Farino and Jakob Schwarz

VISUAL EFFECTS COMMENTARY
by Ernest Farino, Visual Effects Supervisor

"I 've always felt that visual effects are like cinematography or music or any other aspect of making a film. They're one of the tools that help tell the story. So they have to be realistic, but of course, inter-esting, exciting, and dramatic," said "Frank Herbert's Dune" Visual Effects Supervisor Ernest Farino. Farino is both Visual Effects Supervisor and Second Unit Director on location in Prague. His duties included overseeing and coordinating the different people who were working on the large variety of special visual effects which would enhance the live action photography in telling the story of the mini-series.

Ernie Farino received an Emmy nomination for "Outstanding Achievement in Visual Effects" for his work on the HBO mini-series *From The Earth To The Moon*. His other credits include *Starship Troopers* (1998),

Terminator 2: Judgment Day (1991), *Cast A Deadly Spell* (1991), *The Abyss* (1989), and the original *Terminator* (1984). He's been a fan of special effects since childhood when he was inspired by the likes of Ray Harryhausen (*Jason And The Argonauts*) and Willis O'Brien (*King Kong*). It was inevitable that he would contribute to the history of special visual effects himself, and on "Frank Herbert's Dune" he oversaw the work of dozens of visual effects technicians.

"The teamwork on any movie is important," Farino states. "It's almost a cliché, but on a project of this scope that has so many fantastic elements that can so easily go wrong, everything has to really come together. My responsibility is to work with the director, the cinematographer, and the production designer, to plan everything out very carefully so that once we get onto the set we all have a clear idea of what needs to be done. From that point on it's a case of monitoring to make sure there are no unexpected problems."

"There are three visual effects companies providing the principal visual effects for 'Frank Herbert's Dune,' Area 51, Netter Digital, and AI Effects. Then there are some additional companies doing other effects, or matte paintings, including Digital Firepower, E=mc^2 Digital and Title House Digital. Basically the effects companies will take the live action

Alec Newman acting in front of a "green screen"

Riding a sandworm in front of a "green screen"

scenes that we have photographed in Prague, whether it is a 'green screen' or just a normal scene such as a hangar location or on the desert set. They will then process that footage in a way that integrates the images, for instance, of the sandworm, or the Thopter, that they have created in the computer or have animated with the live action footage to make one complete and seamless image.

"It will take approximately eight to nine months to complete all of the visual effects. This includes some of the work that was actually being done while we were still shooting the mini-series such as modeling the worm and the Thopter and various other development work and design work.

"I think the biggest challenge to a project like this," Farino pointed out, "is the fact that you are creating a fully functional science fiction world. That's not to say that hasn't been done before, but nevertheless it still poses considerable challenges and problems given the size and scope of this production. How do you create something that's interesting and different, yet believable enough so that the audience can fully accept this fictional world and enjoy the story?

"I think Kreka did a wonderful job creating the sets and giving us the environment to work with. Now with the visual effects, we add the last elements to Vittorio's beautiful photography and hopefully complete the realization of John's vision for the movie."

A Heighliner

NETTER DIGITAL: LAUREL KLICK
Spaceships, Folding Space, Water of Life Sequence, Dream Imagery

Netter Visual Effects Supervisor Laurel Klick described some of their contributions to "Frank Herbert's Dune." "We're creating all the spaceships and shuttles, and a sequence of shots during the Fremen 'Water of Life' ceremony when Jessica Atreides transforms the water from a drowned worm to become a Reverend Mother."

Designing spaceships for a world twenty-three thousand years in the future that did not look like those in other science fiction films required that new approaches be taken.

"More than anything, the ship designs were defined by going as far away from the *Star Wars* look as we could," Laurel said.

Netter was also responsible for the sequence in which the Navigator folds space and the end of the movie sequence, which has vortexes, cosmic storms and giant tornadoes.

"The Navigator is actually a puppet created by KNB. We are adding its environment and creating the 'folding space' effect," said Laurel.

A four-photo sequence showing a Heighliner folding space.

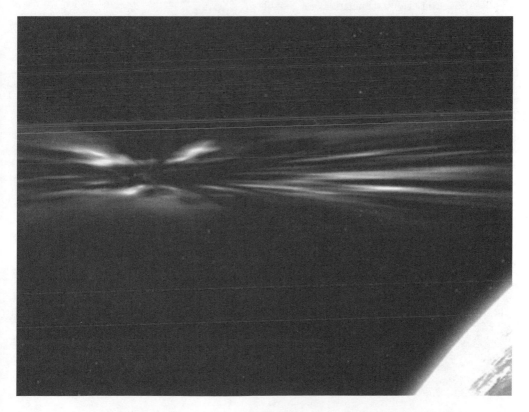

Above and below: the interior of a Heighliner

Lady Jessica in the Water of Life ceremony

Folding space is an unusual effect which they designed from the ground up. "This is a pretty amazing effect. We're interpreting a way of traveling that no one knows for sure what it would actually look like—to have space folding in on itself. We wanted to give the audience a sense of the sky and the atmosphere being sucked in and that everything twists along with the shuttle and then when space unfolds everything comes back to normal in a very organic motion."

Netter Digital Technologies credits include *Impostor, BASEketball, From Dusk Till Dawn, Mousehunt, Mr. Magoo, Babylon 5, Bats, Nutty Professor II, Mystery Men* and the TV mini-series *Storm of the Century.*

The Arrakeen Palace

DIGITAL FIREPOWER & E=mc² DIGITAL
Matte Paintings: Arrakeen Palace, Harkonnen City
Charles Darby and Bob Morgenroth

The visual effects companies Digital Firepower and E=mc² Digital worked to provide composited digital matte paintings of the Arakeen Palace and Harkonnen City. Unlike matte paintings, which for years were painted on glass (in order to be back-lit) or realized with other similar methods, digital matte paintings are done on the computer.

As Bob Morgenroth, Visual Effects Producer for E=mc² explained, "The digital matte painter for 'Frank Herbert's Dune' is Charles Darby of Digital Fire Power. He has established himself as one of the premiere digital matte painters. He did a majority of the paintings of the *Titanic* in the James Cameron film that did not involve animation, such as digital matte paintings of the ship in the harbor."

"Myself and my team at Digital Firepower worked on various concepts for both Harkonnen and Arrakeen, incorporating strong primary colors to better emulate the beautiful production design. Inspired by various sources including William Blake and the architecture of Lebbeas Woods, we formed paintings that were designed to portray the character of those who live in the cities we created," said Charles Darby, Matte Supervisor.

For the Arrakeen Palace and Harkonnen City, Darby started by painting a watercolor of the initial concepts. He and Bob then got together with Visual Effects Supervisor Ernest Farino and Director John Harrison to look at the watercolors.

"The watercolors are done relatively quickly, then John, Ernie, and I would make comments as to what direction things need to go in," Morgenroth explains. "The view, for instance, whether it needs to be closer, or wider or taller or farther away.

"The next stage is making the gray scale illustrations. They're done in black and white and incorporate the changes based on the comments on the watercolors. These images will be scanned into a computer and then digitally embellished with color and detail, ultimately creating the final digital matte painting. The watercolor itself is never used in the actual finished product; it serves as the jumping off point."

While the digital matte paintings were being refined, the earlier, gray scale versions were given to the director to use as "temp shots" during his early editing stages on the project.

"When Digital Firepower finishes the digital matte painting, we take that computer file [which is fairly huge because we're doing this at high definition resolution] and start adding other elements that either we create or Ernie gives us from other visual effects houses and then composite everything into what will be the final shot."

A detail of the Arrakeen Palace

Preparing a Translite for a scene

TITLE HOUSE DIGITAL: CHIP POTTER
Desert Landscape Enhancements, Color Correction
of Scanned Negative

Title House Digital did key scenes intended to establish the important exterior vistas on the desert planet Arrakis using a process called "Landscape Enhancements." The process takes the live action sequences filmed on the sound stages and makes them appear more like real exteriors.

As Chip Potter of Title House Digital explains it, "We're using some very sophisticated 3D packages to create digital landscapes that match the angles of the existing sites that were shot.

Above and below: Translites showing the landscape of Dune

The blank screen in the background will be replaced with a landscape image.

"With the advent of better scanners and higher resolutions, you're now basically able to create a photo montage of what you would like your backdrop to be. You're getting a cross between what the old scenic painters could do, where they would create a realistic backdrop drawn from memory or their artistic skill, and the Translite which is literally a composite of photographs assembled into one giant image.

"The Translites were physically seamless and they were beautifully lit and shot, but there is still limitations to shooting on a stage against a Translite. For instance, in the computer we've incorporated a camera move so that we can start off way out in the horizon, move over, crane down and look at our actors who are walking through the sand that was shot in live action on the sound stage. The result is the creation of huge vistas."

Title House Digital has other highly technical tasks to perform on "Frank Herbert's Dune." They are handling the color correction on the negative that gets scanned for use by all of the visual effects houses. This is a bigger job than it may sound like. That is because cinematographer Vittorio Storaro conceived a unique color palette for the film in which the lighting is not only keyed to specific characters, but to the mood and tone of a scene. In order for this to work the colors must be consistently applied throughout the movie.

Potter said, "What makes the color corrections so interesting is that Vittorio's color sense, and the way that he sees his imagery, is very brilliant. Very saturated. He may start with a scene that's very orange. I mean overly orange, and then we may go to another scene that's in all deep blues and greens. Just really gorgeous stuff. You go so far as to say that the color is almost a character. The result is that the color is helping to tell the story. But in having to deal with that color on a technical side, it's somewhat of a challenge. We have to take the imagery from the film and translate it into computer data and make sure that Vittorio's same choice of color comes up in the computer.

"The main challenge is to maintain the consistency and the look that they've tried so hard to capture."

Note the illusion of vast depth in the Translite.

Lady Jessica performs the "weirding way."

AI EFFECTS
WEIRDING WAY, HUNTER SEEKER,
DEFENSIVE SHIELDS, HOLOVID
Frank Isaacs, VFX Producer A.I.FX

AI Effects, Inc. was formed in 1994 by Frank H. Isaacs and Tony Alderson. The duo have a combined total of over 35 years of visual effects experience in film, television, commercials, special projects, and the new world of computer graphics. Their credits include work on HBO's *From the Earth to the Moon*, *True Lies*, *Terminator II*, *Near Dark*, *Fright Night II*, *Super Mario Bros.*, *The Abyss*, *Coneheads*, *Star Trek-The Next Generation*, *Dracula*, and *The Last Action Hero*. AI is also one of the leading companies involved in stereoscopic imaging.

"Ernie Farino and I go back all the way to Roger Corman's studio out in Venice back in 1979 when we were working on *Galaxy of Terror*," recalled Frank Isaacs. "That's where we met, and in 1983 I supervised my first feature and Ernie came on to assist in doing a lot of the rotoscoping. Since then we've been on quite a number of shows together."

The primary big sequences AI Effects worked on were the hunter-

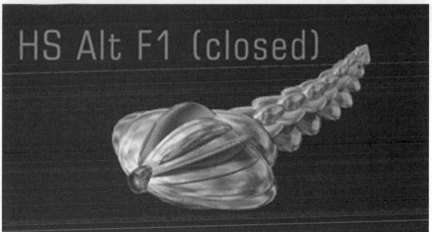

Two views of a deadly Hunter Seeker

seeker, the defensive shields, and the "weirding way" sequences. Their other effects work on "Frank Herbert's Dune" included a holovid shot of Dr. Yueh, all the muzzle blasts, and all the gunfire because they didn't have real working weapons on set. They also did the bulk of the split-screen shots where they take multiple elements that were shot on set and then assemble them into a shot.

The weirding way shots are unusual. "There are three shots, two of Paul and one of Jessica. They have this capability of, in a sense, jumping ahead of real time. Then after they get to where they want to, and turn off the weirding way move, we see multiple images of themselves catch up and get 'absorbed' into them. It's kind of a stutter effect," Isaacs explains, "and it's a very cool effect."

Another effects shot they did involved the Hunter-Seeker, which is the miniature weapon left to try to kill Paul Atreides in his bedroom of the Arrakeen Palace.

"We developed a head for the Hunter-Seeker, and then a segmented body behind it and the whole thing is roughly three inches long" says Isaacs. "The assassin sends this weapon out and it moves on its own propulsion and floats towards its target. Once it is in the room, it senses any movement in the room and it moves to whatever it's tracking. Its mouth opens up. But instead of like our jaw, which only opens with a top and bottom, it opens up in four pieces. Then a needle comes out of the mouth."

The personal defensive shields used by the Atreides and the Harkonnen were also done by AI Effects.

"Ernie wanted the shields to be form-fitting. Almost like a little bubble. It's only up there briefly—just for the time that the mechanism feels that the body is threatened. One of the cool shots is near the end of the sequence when Paul is fighting Gurney. Paul gets an advantage on Gurney and he's slowly putting the knife towards Gurney's throat. When the knife approaches his throat, the bubble forms around Gurney's head and face, but because the knife is moving so slowly, the defensive shield mechanism feels that it's not threatening, and so the shield collapses on itself, and fades away.

"One of the things that is our strength is that we do shots that really become seamless. What Ernie likes is that we make shots look like they're not effects shots."

Combining images to create the Dr. Yeuh hologram. Opposite page: Lady Jessica in front of a table, note that the table is blank; above: Dr. Yeuh (*Robert Russell*) in front of a green screen; below: the Dr. Yeuh hologram image on the table.

A full scale Thopter

AREA 51: TIM McHUGH
Sandworms, Thopters

Area 51 is the company responsible for the shots involving the sandworms and the Thopters. Visual Effects Supervisor and Producer Tim McHugh is the founder of Area 51. Tim's company was brought on to "Frank Herbert's Dune" because he'd worked with Ernie Farino before. "We did *From The Earth To The Moon* together a couple years ago, and that was a great project. That was easy because everything had to look real. There weren't a lot of opinions on what a Mercury capsule has to look like. You just build a Mercury capsule. But with Thopters, sandworms, strange creatures and beasts there's a little interpretation involved. This one has a lot more detail work that we have to go fishing for."

The sandworms and Thopters Area 51 did for *Dune* were all done in Computer Generated Imaging (CGI).

"The crew in Prague built a full scale Thopter which they dragged around on the set for a number of shots," Tim stated. "They built an interior and exterior, and that works for all the live action surrounding shots, but any time you see it fly, or if you see more than one of them on the screen, that would be us."

The Thopter is an unusual aircraft. Short for Ornithopter, Frank Herbert defined it as an aircraft capable of flight by flapping its wings like a bird.

In describing the version seen in the mini-series, Tim McHugh is more detailed in his description of what it is and isn't, and what it can and can't do on screen.

"The Thopter is almost like a giant housefly. We went around and around on the propulsion system. I believe in the book that they actually flap their wings. We did a few tests on that which unfortunately tended to look rather silly, so we modified the design a little bit. What we came up with is something kind of like a vertical take off and landing craft. There's a large spinning propulsion unit in each wing. The two wings tilt up and down independently and reorient themselves in flight as if they are a steering mechanism. So you do see the wings essentially moving, but they do not flap like a bird."

Lady Jessica in front of a wrecked Thopter

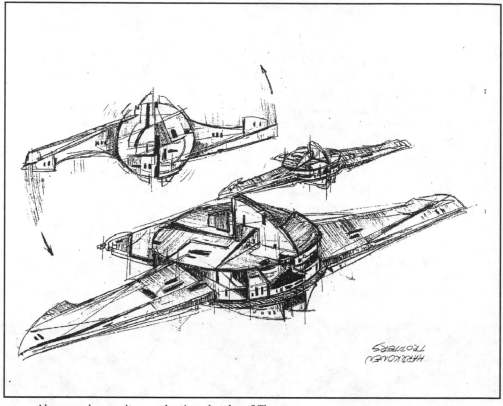

Above and opposite: production sketchs of Thopters

Area 51 also built the Harvester, which is the giant machine that goes out to harvest Spice in the desert.

"We had interesting problems because the difference in scale of the sandworm to the Harvester, to the Thopter and to a human being was so enormous. I told the director John Harrison that it's like trying to put Bambi and Godzilla in the same frame—you tend to shortchange one or the other. So we've had to bring them a little closer to, I hate to call it reality, but so that you could get the same scale. For instance, if we had a worm that was a mile long, which is in the book, just the wake it would create in the sand—you'd see the guys disappear under the sand long before they got anywhere near the worm. So we had to work on that a little bit, and I think we've been successful."

With the sandworms themselves Area 51 tried to come up with something that really looked like a gigantic alien worm, but not like an oversize snake.

"John very much wanted to avoid any kind of snake-like movements on the part of the sandworms," McHugh said.

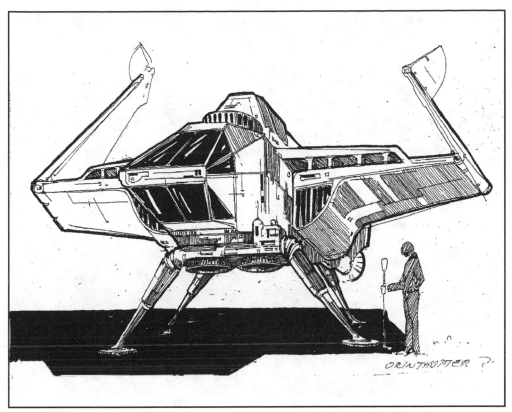

ORINTHOPTER ?

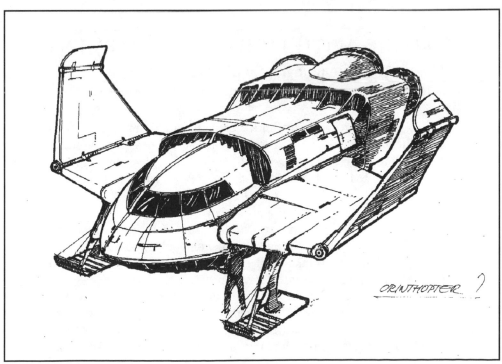

ORINTHOPTER ?

Vittorio Storaro

WRITING WITH LIGHT AND MOVEMENT
The Cinematography of Vittorio Storaro

Vittorio Storaro was born in Italy in June 1940, and his work as a cinematographer is as legendary as the movies he's shot. They include *Apocalypse Now* (1979), *Reds* (1981), *One From The Heart* (1982), *Ladyhawke* (1985), *The Last Emperor* (1987), *Tucker: The Man And His Dream* (1988), *Dick Tracy* (1990), *The Sheltering Sky* (1990), *Little Buddha* (1993), *Bulworth* (1998) and many others.

In describing what it was like working with Vittorio Storaro, director John Harrison said, "It's been a phenomenal experience because Vittorio has been able to take what I created on paper and turn it into a visual feast. The reason I wanted to work with Vittorio was because I've always loved his application of light and color as story elements. Vittorio has made it his career to understand the psychology of color and light, and there's no better project for that than 'Frank Herbert's Dune'."

While some films credit the kind of work he does to the Director of

Photography, Vittorio has very specific reasons why he prefers the des-
ignation of "Cinematographer."

"I say cinematographer, not director of photography, because to me
the meaning of the word is very important. Cinematographer, in my
opinion, means writing with light and movement. I'm trying to write
with light in each movie that I've been called to."

This was not the first time Vittorio had been approached to work on
a motion picture adaptation of *Dune*. In the late 1970s the European
director Jodorowski was mounting a production of the film and he
approached Vittorio to be the cinematographer. Although he really liked
the book, Vittorio chose instead to answer Francis Ford Coppola's call to
film *Apocalypse Now*.

Left to right: Vittorio Storaro, John Harrison, and (far right) Ernest Farino

The decision proved fortuitous as Jodorowski's movie collapsed when the backers decided that science fiction films were not a profitable investment.

Years later, Vittorio crossed paths again with *Dune*. "I was in Los Angeles shooting *Picking Up The Pieces* with First A. D. Matthew Clark," he said. "One day Matthew said, 'Vittorio I'd like to introduce you to a friend of mine. His name is John Harrison. He just wrote a script that came from a book that maybe you know. The book is called *Dune*.' I said, 'What?!' I met with John, and we had a wonderful meeting. We talked about the love that we have for this incredible story, and I showed him what I was doing with Carlos Sara, what I called a revolutionary way to mix the art department and cinematography in order to achieve a new dimension in visual art."

Vittorio and his son Fabrizio create gigantic canvas backdrops called "Translites" that are stretched across the back of a sound stage and are lit from behind to achieve a more realistic effect than one could achieve with a painted backdrop.

Stilgar and Paul Atreides

"These Translites are huge," said John Harrison. "They are designed on the computer using photographs and drawings that we had created. The images are then manipulated, changed, reconfigured, re-colored, put together in numerous different ways and then printed on this huge canvas material which can be lit in a lot of different ways to signify different times of day and different locations.

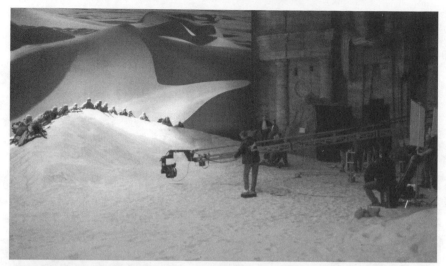

Two scenes from the production

"By integrating these Translites with Kreka's sets, Vittorio was able to design a lighting scheme for each sequence that was never dependent on natural or available light. Color and intensity could change within each scene to enhance the emotional drama, to indicate character change and development, to increase suspense or intensify passion. In short, the production scheme enabled Vittorio to shoot the film in his own, inimitable style.

"Because he was such a knowledgeable fan of the book, we were able to communicate about the storytelling visually in a more profound manner than is usually the case. Every day of pre-production Vittorio and I would meet in my apartment with Matt Clark and Visual Effects Sup-

Vittorio Storaro

ervisor Ernie Farino and literally read through the script scene by scene, to design the movie visually from moment to moment. The result is, I believe, unlike any television event before."

"The Translite backdrop that's been given to us is very exciting," said Saskia Reeves who plays Lady Jessica. "It can be overwhelming sometimes because the sets are so fantastic. Will I be able to be as fantastic as that? It's beautiful what's been done."

In photographing the mini-series, Vittorio conceived an entire thematic program for the use and representation of color. Each major group would be identified and defined by a distinct color—the warm, earth-tone of ocher for the Atreides, violent red for the Harkonnen, blue for the Emperor, green for the Fremen, black for the Bene Gesserit and white for Paul. Color Timer Lou Levinson at Post Logic had the difficult task of color correcting all the richly saturated film that Vittorio shot.

Actor Alec Newman found Vittorio's thematic approach to be a particularly amazing and satisfying one. "Vittorio doesn't just stick a light in and roll the camera. No cinematographer ever does, of course, but he came up with this huge theory for 'Frank Herbert's Dune' and worked with John [Harrison] on a lighting plan for the whole thing. His idea is that *Dune* is basically the journey of Paul Atreides, from the boy who begins the story to enlightenment and the fulfillment of the human soul."

William Hurt found Vittorio's approach particularly rewarding for him in his role of Duke Leto.

"Every scene was an inspiration," Hurt stated enthusiastically. "Vittorio's presence—there's no way you can measure his input. The color schemes he used were all very carefully worked out. He wrote a wonderful amazingly eloquent essay about the use of light and color, and the themes for 'Frank Herbert's Dune'."

While Vittorio has strong views about his work, he recognizes and

Count Fenring and Emperor Shaddam IV

Lady Jessica

appreciates the cooperative effort inherent in filmmaking. "Film is not a single expression," he said. "It is a common expression between the writer, the producer, the actor, the cinematographer, the production designer, the costume designer, the editor, musician; all together, linked and directed by the director, of course. Each one of us is giving some kind of energy into it. And each movie is different because the chemistry is different."

Reflecting on what appealed to him most about the story of "Frank Herbert's Dune," Vittorio said, "The journey of the main character, Paul Atreides, is a symbol. A symbol of the journey for all of us."

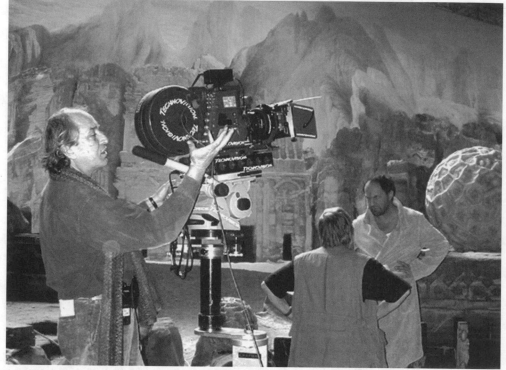

Left: Vittorio Storaro; far right: Uwe Ochsenknecht

CINEMATOGRAPHY IDEATION
OF THE FILM
By Vittorio Storaro

One of the highest periods of the philosophical thought of mankind was certainly the fourth century before Christ: Confucius in China; Buddha in India; Zarathustra in Persia; Socrates, Plato and Aristotle and the whole of the philosophical thought of ancient Greece, certainly laid the bases for a concept of life which for many centuries guided Man along his path of growth until the magic formula of Albert Einstein: $E=mc^2$, placed our Flesh and our Spirit in close connection to the point of projecting us into a future which still today we only manage to perceive through that omnipresent hope of constant growth towards the Evolution of our species

Addressing ourselves to that incredible period of philosophical reflection where Life was seen in terms of the Balance between the FOUR PRIMARY ELEMENTS OF NATURE: WATER, EARTH, FIRE, AIR one could think of seeing the voyage of PAUL ATREIDES as the story of a symbolic Being journeying through the four stages of the life of man, CHILDHOOD, YOUTH, GROWTH, MATURITY which are compared to the four elements of life, in order, at the end of this voyage, to reach that BALANCE which more than anything else belongs to us. Visually one could symbolically represent these four stages with the colors which express them: GREEN, OCHER, RED, BLUE—in order to arrive at the sum of individuals rather than looking at their inner distinctions: feelings, emotions and colors, the WHITE of MATTER made ENERGY. The history of Paul Atreides in "FRANK HERBERT'S DUNE" is thus the history not only of waiting for the Messiah who was so important for all the peoples of the Earth in the past, so fundamental in the present, and certainly indispensable to the Future in order to find the right road for the whole of mankind. The history of Paul also represents—indeed is—the history itself of Man. This time the figure of the Messiah is wanted, sought for, constructed. Paul contains, genetically placed within Him, all the Elements of Life, laid on his shoulders by a specific will to want such a reality. His physical body carries with it the weight of a Destiny built outside his own will. He has before him a path: heavy, felt, lived out: moment after moment, feeling after feeling, emotion after emotion, where he enjoys every element that forms his composition.

The SHADOW from which he emerges is the beginning of everything. His mysterious nature has the power to hide him, protect him, placing him in the UNCONSCIOUS of his own Light. Our innermost SELF spreads out in this darkness seeing it as part of ourselves, but the spirit of Paul, alert, peers into the mystery in which he finds himself every Night and waits trustingly for the draw-

Lady Jessica and Paul Atreides

Paul Atreides (middle) and Fremen riding a sandworm

ing near of every new Dawn. With the perseverance characteristic of great spiritual beings he walks towards this new Light, step after step, towards the word EVOLUTION.

His and our history begins in a time, which is ancient for HIM, from that MATTER in which everything began, from that Unconscious Darkness of the Past that is the MOTHER of all our senses. Ever since ancient times, indeed, It has been seen as the matrix of the elements of nature, the elements which contain the two fundamental substances which make up Life: MATTER and ENERGY— DARKNESS and LIGHT. Man, once he has begun the journey of Matter, from a Past of Darkness passes on to the Present state of twilight to aspire to a Future of Light, towards Energy itself. It will be through going down the long path of the UNCONSCIOUS, the CONSCIOUS, and the SUPERCONSCIOUS that Matter will find the impulse towards its Future belonging in ENERGY. The first stops of the path take place in the great Mother NIGHT where everything is in preparation.

In containing the opposed Elements, which begin the word life, it represents those things, which are beyond our mortal senses. It engenders in Man a reverential state through its protective mysterious potentiality. It is the color of BLACK, of not yet light, which only certain mother figures manage to penetrate, a color which belongs to them because they themselves are Mothers of living matter. It symbolizes the whole of the BENE GESSERIT, a people of Mothers who for some time has been patiently preparing for a future destiny through a specific genetic selection, from woman to woman, from pregnancy to pregnancy, until there comes JESSICA, the last Mother, the Mother of Paul.

And it is with the Light of an AURORA (Pre-Dawn), with the premonition of an arrival, as though emerging from that very thin TWILIGHT which characterizes the PRE-CONSCIOUS, with the rising of the SUN which indicates the move from the UNCONSCIOUS to the CONSCIOUS, that Paul, like the new Christ, is placed in the world. Born from the element WATER, he breaks that amniotic sack which represents the ancient Primary Ocean from which all lives seem to spring. The fertilizing Water of the Soul, the Maternal Element, is identified with Mother Earth; she too is a part of the cycle of the nourishment of life. She is always connected to the MOON, one of the Primordial Elements, sacred to all the cults of humanity. Jessica opens up the rush of the waters with the birth of her first-born son; out of love for the loved, she becomes the Mother of a son she wants now, before the time that he, the *Kwisatz Haderach*, was destined for. From this Element, Paul becomes the leader of a people the FREMEN. This is a community, which for some time has been waiting for Him on the desert planet of DUNE, where Water is almost absent and thus very valuable. For some time waiting for their Messiah, the people of the Fremen are trying to free themselves from the tyrannical oppression of the HARKONNEN, and to follow the teachings of their Prophet, Dr. Kynes, who for some time has been proclaiming the arrival of a leader who will bring about the dream of the transformation of Dune, the reign of the element of Fire, into a Planet in balance with all the other elements, a possible new Arcadia.

(1) WATER represents the spring of DAWN, the element that supports the path of a new Sun. The source which throws light upon the first cry of this new

Feyd

A fight between Fremen and Harkonnen soldiers

child, a shining Awareness which shows itself to the world like a charioteer who drives his chargers and the flaming chariot of Father Sun along the roads between Sky and Earth. It's his CHILDHOOD. In a Light in which INTELLIGENCE itself becomes concentrated, there expands that color which symbolizes this first Element—GREEN. It represents the expansion of awareness of the age of man, connecting the two worlds of the Beginning and the End, of Light and Darkness. It is the color of the Soul; reconciling opposed signs it magically unites the Spirit and Matter. Its chromatic symbol encounters the principle of the lunar planet. It represents Knowledge, Mystery and Destiny. Water, therefore, is the element, which characterizes the FREMEN people.

(2) The EARTH, which brings with it the light of the EARLY MORNING, is the new stage of his life, in which Paul, in a process of continual growth, finds himself living. Represented by the UNIVERSAL MOTHER who nourishes all beings, the protector of human fertility and the beginning of every form of life in the world, the new element has Paul grow up in the warmth of a certain number of Mothers, makes him live his childhood years in the protected security of the paternal figure, in the harmonious and upright discipline of DUKE LETO, in a family which seems to belong to a new Renaissance. The SUN, which follows him constantly from the sky, is for him a symbol of spiritual force, it is CONSCIOUSNESS, the FATHER, the SELF.

Respectfully lost, he sees that he is surrounded by those crowns of Light which are emanated from great spiritual personalities and which increasingly seem to belong to him. The sovereignty of the solar star, symbol of OMNIPOTENCE, leads on to be how illuminates the familial and paternal color of OCHER, the color which in the age of Man represents Growth, the family nucleus. The color of Feeling, of Sensitivity, of Introspection, throws light on the life of Paul from his planet of birth, CALADAN. Colored by so much luminosity, he grows up under the discipline of his Mother, a Bene Gesserit. It is in this chromaticity that He receives the gift of knowledge about the use of his "SENSES," managing through subtle sensorial inflections to sense the behavior of the people who surround him, to know how to "Understand," "Feel," and "See" what awaits him in time. Everything in Him becomes increasingly not only a special figure of the individual being but an image of a PAUL ATREIDES who represents us all.

(3) THE FIRE, which consumes the Light of Life, is the predominant element in which the desert planet of Arrakis receives our protagonist. It is during his period of carefree youth that Paul comes to "see" the infinite sands of DUNE. He arrives there in the highest achievement of Light Consciousness, on his "DAY" which represents the extreme expression of the powerful LUMINOSITY of our earthly existence, the GROWTH. Then, a little later, he enters the AFTERNOON of his life, in the color YELLOW, which proclaims the changing of time. The destroying and liberating element, which dominates this planet, expresses the renewal of a life of both fear and veneration and bears within it the strange capacity for purification. It seems to refer to the inner SPIRIT of Man, with its power of illumination, which consolidates at one and the same time his earthly origins and his celestial destiny. It is in this stage of his journey of life that he comes into conflict with the abuse of power, arrogance, and excessive power of the HARKONNEN. It is through this flaming Element that He comes to know violence, suffering, and pain. The Death of his paternal figure, a Sun which met its SUNSET too early, brings with it the beginning of a decline of creative Energy, and reveals the penetrating thought in Paul's forehead—the possible loss of consciousness. When the dying Sun once again reaches the low sky of the city of Arrakeen, the color which dies this space of his life—RED—acquires an exorcism against impermanence. This color of conflict, as explosive as youthful Blood, is synonymous with power, which is both generative and destructive at the same time. It is a chromatic vibration, which leads to selfishness, to hatred, and to violence. It is the sign of Impulse, of Power, and of Conquest. It is a flame, which throws light on inner desire. Many of Paul's visions are illuminated by this color; flames, blood, dying Light. A color of the tone of the Past which shows Paul not only the violence of his rival, but at the same time illuminates him with regard to his ancestry. He discovers that he is the grandson, through his Mother, of the greatly hated BARON HARKONNEN.

(4) The AIR, like a cosmic breath which identifies with the Word, the intermediate symbol between Fire and Water, is the element in which Paul understands that he has reached the final stage of his life, the MATURITY. Union between Sky and Earth, it is the soul of the world, and allows the falling of the rains, the flowing of the Lands, the flaming of Fire, the blowing of the Winds. It is the spirit, which shapes Matter; it is the Aura of Wisdom, of Prophecy. This aura, in terms of colors, is represented by BLUE, by the color which comes forth with the arrival of EVENING, which, in the sky of DUNE there appear the two MOONS which lift up this planet and surround Paul's head even more than Lights, even more than the Maternal figures.

With the beginning of the empire of the Lunar Light one of the most powerful of energies pushes Paul into the arms of the Unconsciousness of the Night.

The Asteroid, the IMAGO MATER with the mysterious face of a Goddess, is not only the daughter of the night sky but also the Mother of all our most hidden thoughts. Its Light, which is essentially spiritual, is a symbol of matriarchal awareness, it contains a principle of transformation, of resurrection, of immortality. It belongs to the two opposed forces: masculine solar and female lunar, principles that form the union of opposites: Light and Darkness, Life and Death. An evocation of a Vision as nourishment of the Soul.

It is thus in the disturbing feeling of two separate Lights, two separate colors, that Paul discovers that he belongs to two separate Moons, two images of woman which will be at his side during his future life. One of these is CHANI, the daughter of the ideologue-prophet of the natives of Dune—the planetologist KYNES. She is connected with the fascination of the second Moon, the one which shines forth the color GREEN, symbol of itself and of the people to which it belongs. The other is IRULAN, the daughter of the Emperor Shaddam IV, who marks out his imperial path with a luminous Shade of the color VIOLET. She is enveloped in the rays, which come from the first Moon. Her image is unfailingly surrounded by AZURE, the color that brings with it the drawing near of the night, of liberation, of feeling. This is the same color which marks the eyes of the Fremen people, the color that procures the Spice in which all the food of the planet is soaked. Its celestial energy seems to have something higher than Man himself—Silence is probably the right condition for its melancholic beauty. The sensitive feature of this chromatic tonality seems to evoke the reflected image of those human experiences, which are always directed towards ancient depths. It belongs to the colors of the FUTURE.

Only in this way, after passing through all the stages of his life, all the elements, all the feelings, does Paul come to the end of his path. He had started off from the Matter of the Darkness and the Night, but now he comes not only to see but to live his own real representation: the LIGHT. A luminous energy which seems to reach a far away place, and infinite, still to be illuminated. The luminous vibration always waited for, always welcomed, always absorbed, by the whole of humanity, is perhaps the meaning of the existence itself which belongs to us all: ENERGY.

Visible Energy, springing forth from the solar Father, passes through that series of electromagnetic transformations which compensate for the loss of blood by irradiation, from every Sunrise to every Sunset, towards, our own purpose: EVOLUTION. The space filled by its mark in the sky, the Rainbow, is probably a message of love directed towards our destiny. From the birth of RED until the maturity of VIOLET, it fills our lives with luminous sensations, with chromatic Emotions, it makes us feel that we belong to that Energy which, although it is born from Matter, is at the same time its Father, generating with it everything, even Ourselves, becoming our evolutionary purpose, SUPER-CONSCIOUSNESS, the LIGHT.

Only in this way, when Paul manages to see the opposing elements together in the same image of the Sky, the elements of the Sun and the Moon, of the Conscious and the Unconscious, of Man and Woman, does he understand that the accomplishment of the journey of maturation is near. When He feels the vibration of those elements that come together, which balance each other, uniting their strengths, their destinies, and their colors. He can finally reach being, the image of himself, both human and divine at the same time. An achieved BALANCE which is represented visually by the color WHITE of the pure Light of Enlightenment.

This last is the color of Intelligence, together with Knowledge, together with Emotionality; it is the color of ENERGY. It is the color that most represents him at the highest moment of ENLIGHTENMENT, as Paul, as Man, as the Messiah. A complete chromacity which leads the mind towards the perception of Wisdom. It is the color of colors because it contains them all and It exists because it is formed by them all, by their Unity. It is our most intimate desire of achievement, even outside our Awareness. It contains within itself an image of the Absolute, the symbol of the dominion of Energy over Matter.

In this way Paul manages to perceive in his visions the Universe as Infinite, without a beginning and without an end. Only after a long path of counterposition between opposed elements will Man be able to raise himself of the new stage which awaits him, and this is something that Paul knows. He is aware that he is coming to live in a world of separation, suffering that state of loneliness that he seems to counter with Creativity and Love.

This is an achievement that requires a constant set of lives. Only through time will it be possible to attempt to unite those separate worlds in which Paul, like all of us, is engaged in struggle. He is a representation of that Light, of that Will, and of that Intellect which lead Man precisely in the moment of an Intuition, of a Revelation, of an Ideation, etc. . . . to raise himself above the level of the Conscious and the Unconscious and to face the world of the SUPERCONSCIOUS, a new world which confidently awaits our fulfillment.

Harkonnen soldiers in armor

FAMILY ALBUM

Top: left Miro Gabor, middle Ernest Farino; center left to right: John Harrison, Saskia Reeves and Barbora Kodetová; bottom left to right: David Kappes, Alec Newman and Kreka

Top left to right: Vittorio
Storaro, Giancarlo Giannini
and John Harrison; center:
Julie Cox

Top left to right: John Harrison and Barbora Kodetová; center Left to right: Richard P. Rubinstein, John Harrison and Mitchell Galin; bottom left to right: Kreka and Vittorio Storaro

CREDITS

Unit Production Manager	David Kappes	Watermaster	Dan Brown
		Farrah	Tereza Semlerová
First Assistant Director	Matthew Clark	Harkonnen Lieutenant	Mark Huntley
		Man	Rich Gold
CAST		Guild Agent #2	Philip Lenkowsky
Paul Atreides	Alec Newman	Naib #1	Oldrich Navrátil
Jessica Atreides	Saskia Reeves	Naib #2	Jirí Hanák
Duke Leto Atreides	William Hurt	Noble #1	David Forrester
Stilgar	Uwe Ochsenknecht	Noble #2	Zdenek Maryska
Chani	Barbora Kodetová	Harkonnen Soldier #2	Pavel Bezdek
Gurney Halleck	P.H. Moriarty	Lady in Waiting	Anita Durst
Princess Irulan	Julie Cox	Mother Ramallo	Drahomíra Fialková
Alia	Laura Burton	Young Mother Ramallo	Petra Kulíková
Baron Harkonnen	Ian McNeice	Harkonnen Foreman	Jeff Tyler
Feyd	Matt Keeslar	Harkonnen Soldier #3	Martin Hub
Dr. Yueh	Robert Russell	Boy	Jan Cajzl
Dr. Kynes	Karel Dobry	Harkonnen Bodyguard	Petr Vobecky
Emperor Shaddam IV	Giancarlo Giannini	Sardaukar Smuggler	David Fisher
Count Fenring	Miroslav Táborsky	Imperial Soldier	Dave O'Kelly
Otheym	Jakob Schwarz	Fedaykin #1	Greg Linnington
Duncan Idaho	James Watson	Fedaykin #2	Dan Rous
Piter Devries	Jan Unger	Imperial General	Jan Nemejovsky
Rabban	Laszlo Imre Kish	Fremen Leader	Mikulás Kren
Reverend Mother Mohiam	Zuzana Geislerová	Fremen #2	Brian Jaurequi
Thufir Hawat	Jan Vlasák	Officer	Robert Lahoda
Shadout Mapes	Jaroslava	Fremen #3	Ivo Novák
	Siktancová	Other Woman	Petra Lustigová
Servant Women #1	Rianne Kooiman	Puppeteers	Matej Forman
Lieutnent #1	Steve Fisher		Petr Forman
Turok	Noel Le Bon		
Bene Gesserit #1	Elizabeth Sofranco	Stunt Agency FILMKA	
Servant Women #3	Klára Issová	Stunt Coordinators	Ladislav Lahoda
Guard #1	Pavel Vokoun		Petr Drozda Sr.
Spice Spa Attendant	Joel Sugerman	Assistant Stunt	
Lingar Bewt	Jeff Caster	Coordinators	Katerina Lahodová
Esmar Tuek	Pavel Kríz		Pavel Bezdek
Guild Rep	David Máj	Stunt doubles	David Motl
Sardaukar Captain	Pavel Cajzl		Hana Dvorská
Harkonnen Soldier #1	Robert Jaków		Martin Hub
Fremen #1	Petr Vacek		Dusan Hyska
Bene Gesserit #2	Clotilde Le Grand		Petr Vlasák
Jamis	Christopher Lee Brown	Assistant Producer	Michael Messina

Production Supervisor	Michelle Weller
Unit Production Manager CZ	Pavel Solc
First Assistant Director CZ	Jirí Ostry
Second Assistant Director	Andy Howard
Prague Casting	Nancy Bishop
London Casting	Wendy Brazington
German Casting	Cornelia von Braun
Dialogue Coach	Nancy Bishop
A–Camera Operator	Alfredo Betro
B–Camera Operator	Ervín Sanders
Focus Pullers	Antonín Marík
	Ladislav Hruby
	Marek Prokes
Clappers/Loaders	Zdenek Mrkvicka
	Zbynek Kunc
	Piernicola di Muro
	Filip Majer
Video Assist	Fabrizio Storaro
	Willy Murgolo
Art Directors	Branimir Babic
	Michal Krska
Set Decorator	Vladislav Lasic
Leadman	Michal Pokorny
Set Designers	Mladen Lisavac
	Miodrag Miric
	David Tichy
	Adam O'Neill
Translite Images	Fabrizio Storaro
Construction Managers	Vladimír Planansky
	Michal Sula
	Roman Synek
Stand-by Construction	Jaroslav Fiala
	Jaromír Vaverka
Property Master	Karel Vanásek
Propmen	Vladimír Kvech
	Milan Bábik
	Milan Janostík
	Petr Matous
	Karel Jílek
Gaffers	Filippo Cafolla
	Andy Arnautov
Rigging Gaffer	Václav Cermák
Best Boy Electric	Jan Boruvka
Electricians	Borivoj Klecka
	Igor Jelen
	Jirí Horych
	Tomás Jurásek
	Josef Válka
	Bohumil Kapek
	Roman Matrka
Lightboard Operator	Fabio Caffolla
Key Grip	Mauro Diamanti
Grips	Jirí Gazda
	Stefan Stefanov
	Karel Charvát
Crane Operator	Jan Pous
Sound Mixer	Michal Holubec
Boom Operator	Roman Rigo
Special Effects Supervisor	Jim Healy
Special Effects Coordinator	Pavel Ságner
Special Effects Technicians	Roman Tudzaroff
	Rudolf Tudzaroff
	Keith Suzuki
	Russell Hurlburt
Third Assistant Director	Frantisek Rezek

Runners / Ads	Petr Drozda Jr.
	Sibyla Binárová
	Radoslav Cichon
Assistant Costume Designer	Jan Pistek
Key Costumer	Zuzana Máchová
Costumers	Mária Hubácková
	Marie Charvátová
	Zuzana Bursíková
	Dana Bártová
Chief Make-up Artist	Josef Lojík
SFX Make-up	René Stejskal
Assistant Make-up Artists	Nora Robertson
	Ivo Strangmüller
	Milan Vlcek
	Alena Lojíková
	Eva Vyplelová
	Tamara Koubová
	Zdena Prchlíková
Choreographer	Michal Caban
Extras Casting Director	Jirí Hrstka
Extras Casting Assistant	Jaroslav Zizka
Stand-Ins	Lukás Bárta
	Phil Seeger
	Mariana Krenová
Unit Manager	Pavel Typolt
Production Coordinator	Jana Veselá
Assistant Production	
Coordinator (CZ)	Markéta Danková
Assistant Production	
Coordinator (USA)	Erynn Midwall
Erynn Midwall	
Production Accountant	Sheila Allen
First Assistant Accountant	Jessica Stoltz
Assistant Accountants	Lenka Sadílková
	Vladimír Svestka
Cashier	Irena Frycová
Script Supervisor	Lori Wyant
Set Production Assistant	Darko Stavrik
Office Production Assistant	Lenka Rock
Assistant to David Kappes	Alisa Moore Buckley
Assistant to Michelle Weller	Lukás Síma
Assistant to John Harrison	Tricia Deering
Assistant to William Hurt	
(USA)	Wendy Wasdahl
Assistant to William Hurt	
(CZ)	Klára Holubová
Interpreters	Dennis Todorovic
	Andrea Kerlická
	Stepánka Rocková
Location Manager	Aneta Valásková
Location Assistant	Halina Himmelová
Catering	Catering Petricard 2000 s.r.o.
Medics	Martin Supka
	Dita Lylová
	Markéta Reichlová
Still Photographer	Zdenek Vávra
Transportation Coordinator	Gabriela Dolenská
Drivers	Václav Matejka
	Milan Zíka
	Karel Beran
	Radek Lehoucka
	Antonín Korenek
	Pavel Rados
	Jaroslav Církva Sr.

Milan Schlinz
Pavel Holub
Frantisek Kafka
Vilém Danek
Václav Kocman
Josef Havlícek
Jaroslav Církva Jr.
Zbynek Svoboda
Jaroslav Kouba
Vladimír Horky
Jirí Myslivec
Bohumil Machácek
Frantisek Flosman

2nd UNIT	
Director	Ernest Farino
Unit Manager	Michal Cerveny
First Assistant Director	Larry Horricks
Second Assistant Director	Richard Gironi
Runners / AD	Helena Franková
	Tereza Engelová
	Zuzana Smuková
Director of Photography	Miro Gábor
Camera Operator	Martin Benc
Focus Pullers	Libor Bruha
	Ivan Simunek
	Lenka Dimitrovová
Clappers/Loaders	Marek Schnierer
	Stanislav Vales
Video Assist	Viktor Lonek
Stand-by Construction	Miroslav Mráz
	Vladimír Pribyslavsky
Propmen	Martin Divic
	Zbynûk Chvojka
Gaffer	Andy Arnautov
Best Boy Electric	Jirí Curin
Electricians	Zdenek Cermák
	Josef Cernusák
	Ladislav Marek
	Michal Sroubek
Lightboard Operator	Danielle Caffolla
Key Grip	Ivo Gresák
Grip	Jindrich Hanzel
Sound Mixer	Petr Forejt
Boom Operator	Jana Smídová
Costumers	Marta Jencová
	Helena Rovná
	Bela Friedlová
Assistant Make-up Artists	Jirí Budín
	Dana Kohoutová
Stand-in	Michal Supka
Script Supervisor	Laura Siváková
Set Production Assistants	David Adam
	Daniel Sklenár
Medic	Anicka Hríbalová
Still Photographer	Petr Rosicky
Drivers	Petr Zlatnik
	Josef Dlabac
	Jirí Oplustil
Associate Producer	Harry B. Miller III
First Assistant Editor	Andrea Folprecht
Assistant Editor	Elvio Sordoni
Apprentice Editor	Adrian Colon

Visual Effects Coordinator (Prague)	Gary Beach
Visual Effects Coordinator (Los Angeles)	Sarah Coatts
Visual Effects Editor (Prague)	Martin Hubácek
Visual Effects Editor (Los Angeles)	Linda Drake
Spacecraft Design	Jim Bandsuh
Storyboards	John Zurbo
Miniatures Cinematography	Tony Cutrono
Miniatures Production Manager	Carlyle Livingston
Sound Supervisor	Jay Wilkinson
ADR Supervisor	RJ Palmer
Sound Editors *	Victor Iorillo
Music Editor	Josh Winget
Orchestrator	Tim Simonec
Sound Editing Facility	Miles O'Fun
Dubbing Facility	Westwind Media
Special Creature Effects by	Kurtzman, Nicotero & Berger EFX Group, Inc.
Supervisors	Howard Berger
	Greg Nicotero
Key Sculptor	Alex Diaz
Key Mechanics	Luke Khanlian
	Dave Wogh
Additional Mechanics	Mark Hull
	Jake Mckinnon
Lab Technicians	Chad Atkinson
	Steve Hartman
	Alex Lorenzana
	Brian Rae
Production Manager	Kamar Bitar
Coordinator	Chizuru Hasegawa
Purchasing	Linda Bastin
Visual and Digital Effects	Area 51
Visual Effects Supervisor	Tim McHugh
Digital Compositing Supervisor	Glenn Campbell
Digital Efftects Supervisor	Scott D. Wheeler
Visual Effects Coordinator	Michelle Massie
Visual Effects Animators	Kevin Gendreau
	Jim Hofman
	Don L. McCoy
	Chris Q Zapara
Systems Manager	Jake Jacobson
Visual Effects by	Netter Digital Entertainment, Inc.
Visual Effects Supervisor	Laurel Klick
Visual Effects Executive Producer	Jason Netter
Visual Effects Producer	Susan Norkin
Visual Effects Coordinator	Elaine Essex Thompson
Lead Compositor	Martin Hilke
Compositors	Beverly Bernacki
	Steve Caldwell
	Michael Pecchia
Animators	Clay Dale
	Wayne England
	Paul Grimm
	Steve Graves
	John Savage
	Gina DiBari
Modelers	Andrew Harlow

	Ryan Dauner
	Ryan Carter
	Justin Knowles
	Tim Petre
	Igor Pinevich
	Robert Ward
Editorial Assistant	Ryan Gomez
Systems Administrator	Jose Arrendondo
Data Manager	Brenda Finster
Special Visual Effects by	AI Effects, Inc.
Visual Effects Supervisor	Frank H. Isaacs
Digital Effects Supervisor	Tony Alderson
Lead Digital Animator	Michael F. Hoover
Digital Animators	Cecilia Cosintini
	Jay Banks
Digital Visual Effects by	Flat Earth Productions, Inc.
	Doug Beswick
	Kevin Kutchaver
	Kevin OiNeill
Visual Effects Coordinator	Russel Johnson
3D Supervisor	Everett Burrell
Digital Matte Artist	Philip Carbonaro
3D Modeling	Kevin Struckman
	John Gibbons
Digital Matte Painting Composites	E=mc2, Inc.
Visual Effects Supervisor	Bob Morgenroth
Digital Matte Artist	Charles Darby, Digital Firepower
CGI Supervisor	Paul LeBlanc
Digital Painting Burbank Division	Laser Pacific Media Corp.
Operations	Dave Parkinson
Digital Landscapes *	Title House Digital
"Baron" Rig Removal	Proxima S.R.L.
Visual Effects Supervisor	Fabrizio Storaro
Digital Effects Supervisor	Gianluca Rizzo
Digital Artist	Gianluca Risita
Post Production Accounting	Owen & Desalvo
Post Production Facilities	Technicolor Rome
	Laser Pacific Media Corporation
Colorist	Lou Levinson, Post Logic Studios

Editing Equipment Provided by	Edit Hire
	Edit Point
Shipping	Alberto Ferri, Rome
	Film Sped, Prague
Construction	Barrandov Studio, divize
Dekorace	
	Michal Sula, MS – Dekor Gatteo
Stages	Barrandov Studios, Czech Republic
	Milk & Honey Studios, Letnany, Czech Rep.
Motor Homes	Vladimír Horky
Consultant	Brian Herbert
Prague Accomodations	Hotel Blue Key
	Hotel Na Kampe 15
Negative Cutter	RPG Productions Inc.
	Rick Gordon
	Frances Solis
	David Palomares
	Tom Kugler
Unit Publicist	Larry M. Garrison
EPK Photography	J.R. Hall
Business Affairs for Victor Television	Lee Rierson, Esq.
Production Legal	Rosalind Lawton, Esq.
Legal services CZ	Dr. Vladimír Kroupa
Representing Betafilm	Moritz Von der Groeben
	Klaus Zimmermann
Representing Tandem Communications	Rola Bauer
	Torsten Dewi
	Sigrid Bachert
	Tim Halkin
Production Services Provided by	Milk & Honey Films, s.r.o. Prague, Czech Rep.
Logo Art	Fabrizio Storaro/ In Visible Inc.
Grip & Lighting Equipment	Panther Prague Noon Filmtechnik, Prague
Film Stock Provided by	Kodak Rome
Special Light by	Iride S.R.L.

Cameras and lenses provided by TechnoVision France

The characters and events depicted in this photoplay are ficticious. Any similarity to actual persons, living or dead, is purely coincidental.

Country of first publication: United States of America. Victor Television Productions, Inc. and Betafilm GmbH are the authors of this motion picture for purposes of the Berne Convention and all national laws giving effect thereto.

A New Amsterdam® Entertainment, Inc. production in association with Victor Television Productions, Inc. and Betafilm GmbH

Please note these credits are tentative as of 7/31/00 and are subject to change. A * symbol indicates more specific information not available at press time.